Edward Augustus Jenks

The Spinning-Wheel at Rest

Poems

Edward Augustus Jenks

The Spinning-Wheel at Rest
Poems

ISBN/EAN: 9783744704731

Printed in Europe, USA, Canada, Australia, Japan

Cover: Foto ©Thomas Meinert / pixelio.de

More available books at **www.hansebooks.com**

The Spinning-Whee

At Rest

THE SPINNING-WHEEL AT REST

POEMS

BY

EDWARD AUGUSTUS JENKS

ILLUSTRATED

Simonides said a picture was dumb poesie, and poesie
a speaking picture.
HOLLAND, tr. of Plutarch

BOSTON
LEE AND SHEPARD PUBLISHERS
10 MILK STREET
1897

ENGRAVING AND PRINTING
REPUBLICAN PRESS ASSOCIA
CONCORD, N. H.

O great-heart shadow-forms of long ago!
    Sweet friends who loved me—now beyond the blue!
You cannot see or hear me, well I know:
    Yet still I hand these evening flowers to you.

And you whose feet still linger at my side,
    Whose love refreshes me like morning dew
And stays the shadows of life's eventide,
    I dedicate these curfew chimes to you.

Never did Poesy appear
So full of heaven to me, as when
I saw how it would pierce through pride and fear
To the lives of coarsest men.
LOWELL.—*An Incident in a Railroad Car.*

PREFACE

IN preparing this volume for the press, the author felt that he
might almost as well go into an October woods, sweep up the
crisp leaves that carpet its solemn crypts, and try to replace them
in living beauty upon the bare arms of the beeches and maples, as
to undertake to bring these wanderers home again. But certain
occult influences, singularly in accord with some subterranean cur-
rent of his own thought, have encouraged him to complete the
work. After all, he is rather glad to welcome his children to his
fireside once more.

At the end are a few notes, referred to by numbers in the body
of the book.

E. A. J.

CONCORD, New Hampshire.

I am satisfied if it cause delight; for delight is the chief, if not the only, end of poesy: instruction can be admitted but in the second place; for poesy only instructs as it delights.

DRYDEN—*Def. of Essay on Dram. Poesy.*

To render poetry by the voice and seize it by the ear, exacts an almost sacred attention. There must exist between the reader and his hearers the closest bond, without which the electric communication of feeling cannot take place. If this cohesion of souls is lacking, the poet is like an angel trying to sing the hymns of heaven amid the sneers of hell.

BALZAC—*Lost Illusions.*

CONTENTS

9

CONTENTS

LIST OF ILLUSTRATIONS

11

THE SPINNING-WHEEL AT REST.

ORPHÈE

POEMS

ORPHEAN MUSIC

THE legendary Orpheus and his lyre,—
Who led the wood-nymphs captive at the sound
Of his clear voice and sentient strings, and bound
The streams with bands so soft they could not tire,
Thrilling the sylvan wilds with sweet desire
To staunch for aye the ever-bleeding wound
Left by his lost Eurydice,—are found
Again when soft October's leafy fire
Burns on the silent mountains, and the woods
Are bursting with the melody that springs
From hidden chambers—chauntings low and
deep,
Fit music for these sacred solitudes.
Here, breathless, all things listen as he sings,
And, listening, fall like children into sleep.

GOING AND COMING

GOING—the great round Sun,
  Dragging the captive Day
Over behind the frowning hill,
  Over beyond the bay—
    Dying :
Coming—the dusky Night,
  Silently stealing in,
Wrapping himself in the soft, warm couch
  Where the golden-haired Day had been
    Lying.

Going—the bright, blithe spring :
  Blossoms ! how fast ye fall,
Shooting out of your starry sky
  Into the darkness all
    Blindly !
Coming—the mellow days ;
  Crimson and yellow leaves ;
Languishing purple and amber fruits
  Kissing the bearded sheaves
    Kindly !

Going—our early friends ;
  Voices we loved are dumb ;

Footsteps grow dim in the morning dew ;
  Fainter the echoes come
      Ringing :
Coming to join our march—
  Shoulder to shoulder pressed—
Gray-haired veterans strike their tents
  For the far-off purple west,
      Singing !

Going—this old, old life ;
  Beautiful world ! farewell !
Forest and meadow ! river and hill !
  Ring ye a loving knell
      O'er us !
Coming—a nobler life ;
  Coming—a better land ;
Coming—the long, long, nightless day ;
  Coming—the grand, grand
      Chorus !

UNDER THE TREES

THE mellow music of this dewy autumn eve
    Tinged with the purple clusters of the bosky vine,
Falls soothingly upon the ear, as on the heart
    The healing benison of sacramental wine.

The while light fingers wake the subtle harmonies
    That sleep among the swaying branches overhead,
We'll watch the unseen angels pave the sky with stars,
    O'er which the phantom coursers of night's Queen will
        tread.

E'en now we hear her wheels behind the breathless hills ;
    And see ! heraldic lights go shooting up the sky :
She comes ! With queenly grace she guides her foaming
        steeds,
    Dispensing regal gifts, love beaming in her eye.

A shower of silver coin falls gleaming at our feet,
    Struck from the leafy dies that swing above our heads ;
And sweetly tired Nature breathes her evening prayer
    Beneath the filmy sheet the mild Queen-mother spreads.

THE OLD STONE BRIDGE[1]

I ENVY you, old Bridge!
    To stand upon the border
Land of shadow, rock, and river,
Where the burnished sun-spears quiver
Forever and forever,
    And the song to the old warder
Endeth never—endeth never!
Ah! I envy you, old Bridge!

I envy you, old Bridge!
    Oh! how the waters sparkle
As they whelm your feet with kisses!
E'en the constellation Pisces
Scarce could blaze with warmer splendor!
    Then to see the waters darkle
With a sadness sweet and tender
As they pass beyond the Bridge!

I envy you, old Bridge!
    You never tire of gazing
At the fishes, deftly speckled,
At the ledges, sunshine freckled,

23

THE OLD STONE BRIDGE

Nor of listening to the trebles,
  So sweet and so amazing,
Of the water on the pebbles.
Yes! I envy you, old Bridge.

ON THE ROAD

THEY wondered how the day could be so bright—
   Those two disciples—and their hearts so sore :
They wondered how the birds could sing—how light
   Could ever shine again on sea or shore.

The way was long—their tear-hung eyes were dim ;
   Their hearts were broken—Faith and Hope had fled ;—
But as they walked, they thought and talked of Him
   Who yesterday lay still among the dead.

The two—oh, wonder !—were increased to three :
   How oft it happens, when our loving thought
Has stretched across an intervening sea
   Of time or space, it brings the friend we sought.

The heart-sore travellers were increased to three :
   Just how it happed those brave hearts never knew ;—
They knew that they were blind—now they could see,
   While words of comfort fell like falling dew.

" Abide with us !" " And he went in." How sweet
   To know that when we open wide the door,
We shall not wait to hear His coming feet,
   But He will sup with us forevermore.

THE DISCOVERY

I AM not young, nor am I very old;
    But Maud is young, and beautiful, and sweet.
My eyes are gray, but not the kind called cold;
    Not cold, at least, when gray and brown eyes meet.
For sometimes, when she lays her soft white hand
    Upon my shoulder, and I clasp her waist,
The sternest anchorite could not withstand
    Her luscious beauty, nor forbear to taste.

I am not very old, I said;—but wait!
    Behind all this there 's something must be told:
Perhaps I 'm passing on with steadier gait
    Than I imagined to the years called "old."
So to the point: 'T was only yesterday
    That, standing at my window looking west,
I saw the tired Sun lay himself away
    On pillows fiery as the hangbird's breast:

I stood and watched him, dreaming all the while
    Of that fair face beset with golden rings,
And of some far-off, dim, enchanted isle,
    And airy palaces and queens and kings,—
When suddenly the door flew open wide
    And all the gathering twilight fled away,

26

For Maud came tripping lightly to my side,
    Like perfumed sunbeams to the fields of May.

My arm stole round her, and her sweet brown eyes
    Raised their long lashes to my bending face,
When all at once there flashed a bright surprise
    From out those ambushed depths of maiden grace :
" Oh, Love !" she cried, " I see a silver thread—
    A gleam of winter—in your tawny beard !
I 'll smother it with molten gold," she said :
    Her head bent low—the silver disappeared.

DANDELIONS

"'GOLD in my pocket!' girlie mine? Oh, no—oh,
    no!—not I!
But I can show you where the pretty golden eagles
    lie
As thick as lighted candles in a summer evening sky.

"Come! there's my little finger! You must hold on
    snug and tight
While we go romping down the lane.——There! stop
    just here!——How bright
They gleam among the soft green grasses! Left, and
    front, and right

"Their yellow laughter greets us, and the speaking
    disks of gold
Look up confidingly—just sweet—not pert, nor over-
    bold:
The Horn of Plenty shook them over all the waiting
    wold.

"But some bright morning, when you hear the early
    robins call,
There'll be no gleaming gold—instead, a spindle, hol-
    low, tall,
And perched upon its breezy top a fuzzy silver ball—

" Each ball a silver quiver full of silver javelins,
Just large enough for fairy queens to hurl at fairy sins—
Or fairies use, in fastening their hats or scarfs, as pins !

" A morning breath will scatter them, and on the wind's
    soft wings
The golden eagles fly away, and all the silver things :
So bright illusions always fade—like promises of kings."

"A MILITARY GENTLEMAN," BY REM-
BRANDT

AN iron face, remorseless, grim, and cold;
   An eye as piercing as the gleaming sword
His mighty arm hath swung when battle rolled
   Its thunderous tide along; a voice that roared
Fierce songs and battle-cries in hot pursuit
   Of flying foes; a mouth as strange to love
And all sweet offices, as heavenly fruit
   To lips of angels fallen from above.

Rembrandt! thy matchless hand and eye are dust:
   "A military gentleman" unknown:
No more his vengeful, stalwart arm will thrust
   The ruthless sabre to the quivering bone,—
But on thy canvas, darker grown with years,
Still lives the shadow of uncounted tears.

WHISPERS

ONE sunny summer afternoon,
When lazy lay the languid moon
  Upon the rocking main,
Though buried deep in sagest books,
No light but gleams from pebbly brooks
  Flashed through my aching brain.

My hat of straw, with tattered crown,
From rusty nail looked kindly down,
  And waved its silken band ;—
Soft music floated on the air ;
A breezy finger touched my hair,
  And cooled my fev'rish hand.

Across the lawn, and by the well
Whose dripping water joyous fell
  Back to its darkling nest ;
O'er meadows shorn, through witching glade,
I sought the silver poplar's shade,
  And laid me down to rest.

A breezy finger touched my eyes—
They closed upon the azure skies ;
  But whispers from above
Came trembling from the silver leaves,

As, when a child its mother grieves,
  She pleads her tender love.

" O wandering brook ! will you not stay
Awhile beneath my shade to-day,
    And, roaming, tell me why ?
For years I 've pressed your mossy bank,
And of your bounty freely drank,
    Yet still you rimple by !"

The water o'er the polished stones
Went flashing on—but answering tones
    Came from its shining way :
" I cannot stay, O gracious tree !
A thousand tongues are calling me,
    And gladly I obey.

" Since dreamy midnight fled before
The op'ning of yon orient door,
    I 've wandered far and wide :—
The meadows quaff my brimming cup :
Wild flowers in troops come springing up,
    And linger at my side.

" The swallow tastes my limpid breast :
The sparrow builds her leafy nest
    Among my dancing plumes,
And whispers to me as I pass,—
While all the wild flowers in the grass
    Are offering me perfumes.

34

WHISPERS

" All nature woos—— Ah ! there 's my joy !
A barefoot, curly-headed boy
   Awaits me on the sand ;
A maiden, too, with soft brown hair,
And form and face supremely fair—
   I 'll kiss—her——tiny———"

The voice was lost among the trees ;
The poplar shivered in the breeze ;
   A leaf came toppling down,
And roused me from my dreamy bed,
With beads of dew upon my head
   Like gems in kingly crown.

THE LAND OF SLEEP

ETERNAL Silence! World forever dumb!
   Ten thousand æons lie within thy cold,
   Inexorable arms ;—and they enfold
Rich argosies of human lives, that come
From out thy frigid breast into the hum
   And fever of our thought, with wealth untold
   Of Arctic secrets—nevermore. Bells tolled,
Unheard, their exit ; and the muffled drum
      Of soundless under-heaving waters rolled
         Its sullen, ice-cold music through the vast
            Unsympathetic waste of frozen breath
         That spans the brazen Northland, when the bold
            True hearts grew strangely still, and, shudd'ring,
               passed
            Into the bosom of this double death.

36

WHO WOULD STAND STILL.

OH ! it is beautiful—this growing old !
  Who would stand still !
E'en while the Morning bathes herself in gold,
  The Sun climbs up the hill.

Who would stand still ! The world we live in spins
  Along the ways
Worn smooth by thundering ages, and begins
  To show her length of days.

We must not gaze upon the backward way
  With vain regrets :
Bright pictures mingle with the evening's gray—
  A few sad silhouettes.

Only the old have store of memories :
  Their wistful ears
Are trained to hold the splendid melodies
  And songs of other years.

And every step they take—each silver hair—
  But marks the near
And yet still nearer day, when over there
  The white tents disappear.

37

One bugle call—and then the glad discharge !
  Just think of it !
To *know* you stand upon the river's marge—
  The very brink of it !

O boyhood's friend !—that only yesterday
  Exhaled like mist—
You seemed in sweet content to float away
  On waves of amethyst :

And howsoever bright this dear old world
  May seem to be,
The best is where last evening's sunset furled
  Its saffron sails for thee.

THE RETURN[2]

"THREE years! I wonder if she 'll know me:
    I limp a little, and I left one arm
At Petersburg, and I am grown as brown
    As the plump chestnuts on my little farm ;
And I am shaggy as the chestnut-burs,
But ripe and sweet within, and wholly hers.

" The darling, how I long to see her !
    My heart outruns this feeble soldier pace ;
For I remember, after I had left,
    A *little* Charlie came to take my place.
Ah, how the laughing three-year-old brown eyes—
His mother's eyes—will stare with pleased surprise !

" I 'm sure they 're at the corner watching ;
    I sent them word that I should come to-night ;—
The birds all know it, for they crowd around,
    Twittering their welcome with a wild delight :
And that old robin with a halting wing,—
I saved her life three years ago last spring.

" Three years ! Perhaps I am but dreaming,
    For, like the Pilgrim of the long ago,
I 've tugged a weary burden at my back,
    Through summer's heat and winter's blinding snow,

Till now I reach my home, my darling's breast,
Where I can throw my burden off—and rest."

    *   *   *   *   *   *

When morning came, the early rising Sun
  Laid his light fingers on a soldier sleeping
Where a soft covering of bright green grass
  Over two lowly mounds was lightly creeping.
But waked him not ;—his was the rest eternal,
Where the brown eyes reflected love supernal.

HER TWELFTH BIRTHDAY

IN that far land where Jordan's silver stream
    Rolls onward, pensive, to the silent sea,
Dwelt Mary, lovely as an angel's dream,—
    The sweetest flower that bloomed in Galilee.

So beautiful was she, so queenly fair,
    So full of purity and heavenly worth,
The Father chose her from the maidens there
    To be the one beloved of all the earth.

———

In the sweet vale where Sugar River sings
    Its love-songs to the music of the bells,
And all the throbbing air is full of wings
    Of bees and birds, another Mary dwells :

My Mary—darling of her father's heart,
    The centre of a thousand hopes and fears :
O Son of Mary ! haste to take her part
    When I have passed the Gateway of the Years.

43

JUNE FANCIES

ON turning the leaves of my memory
      I found a wonderful June,
Where the leaves were as green as its hills were blue ;
Where the birds were as blithe as their vows were true ;
Where the humming-bird and the bumble-bee
Made music as sweet as sweet could be—
      A tremulous, wing-born rune—
That comes floating to me on this breezy knoll
As the flood-tides of memory over me roll.

In that wonderful June of the haze-clad years,
That thirty springs have embalmed in tears,
            I dreamily strolled
            Through a forest old
To a home where the lights and shadows lay
'Neath the swaying boughs the live-long day :
For there the Queen of the forest shades,
The wild flowers twined in her mazy braids,
Held daily court in her breezy castle,
And a loving heart for her trusty vassal.

But I stopped a beechen tree beneath
To list to the music the green woods breathe
            From every dell of the wildwood,
            Where the breezy swells
            Make the billowy bells
Ring soft in the ears of childhood,—

And the rising and falling tide of green
That laved the cliffs of the blue unseen
    Unshipped my soul from its moorings.
So, lying beneath that old beech tree,
In the wine-dark depths of that summer sea,
    My spirit rose on its poor wings
        Through countless fathoms
        Of leafy chasms,
        To where a boat
        Had chanced to float
    From the mystic realm of phantasms.

In that gossamer barque, by the world unseen,
On the surging waves of that sea of green,
    Swinging and singing,
    Singing and swinging,
    Floating along in the ambient air,
I gathered the forest dreams to my breast
Till my soul was full of the strange unrest—
The dancing and tossing and gleaming boughs,
The whispered songs and the whispered vows—
    That greeted me everywhere.

The sun was rollicking down the west,
Proud as a girl in a scarlet vest,
When I anchored above the staid old tree
Where I left myself when I went to sea.

    Down through the dim aisles
    And over the rocks,

Climbing the old stiles,
    And threading the walks
Which the steady tramp of the thirsty kine
Had left in many a tortuous line
Down to the puncheon broad and deep,
Where the hills deposit the wine they weep,—
Where the lilies drink themselves into dreams
Of scintillant wings by the babbling streams,—
    And at waning day
    My devious way
Had led to the marge of the shadowy bay.

On the magic mirror's circling brim
The veeries were singing their evening hymn,—
But hushed their song, as in days of yore
When all the world was entranced before
The beauteous Eve, in her heaven-born dress,
A vision of new-world loveliness ;
For a form delicious as Eden graced,
Half hid by the ripples that kissed her waist,
Was sporting there in the amber water—
The sun and the greenwood's fairest daughter.

I turned aside to a pathway old
    Full of the wondrous vision,
And met my love in the vanishing gold,
    Roaming the fields elysian.
What followed there I dare not tell :
    But it was a grand old tune
Which the green leaves sang,—and they sang it well,—
    In that wonderful evening in June.

— Where has the drink taken us this time? —

SPEED THE GOING—WELCOME THE COMING

Vicksburg, Miss., January 1, 1869

LAST night the calm, sweet Moon looked down
    and wept
To see the Old Year—tottering, patient, pale—
    Slow toiling toward the town while others slept;—
His " frosty pow " no kindly covering wore:
    His silver locks the rudest night winds tossed,
And snatched his staff,—the icicle he bore,—
    Out of the fingers stiffened with the frost.
Alone, deserted, friendless, houseless, cold,
    Unpitied and unloved he seemed to be,
Who once was young and beautiful and bold
    As e'er was rover on the untamed sea.

Well we remember with what ringing cheers
    He coasted down the snow-clad early days,
To find his curly head all drenched with tears
    The blue-eyed Spring-time wept at Love's delays;
And how he wantoned with the birds and bees,
    And kissed the blossoms till their cheeks were flushed
With ecstasy of love and Love's decrees:
    And then, with all their blissful passion hushed
Into the twilight of a perfect peace,
    The young Year glided out beneath the stars,

49

Shrugging his shoulders at his quick release.
And with one bound cleared all the Summer bars!

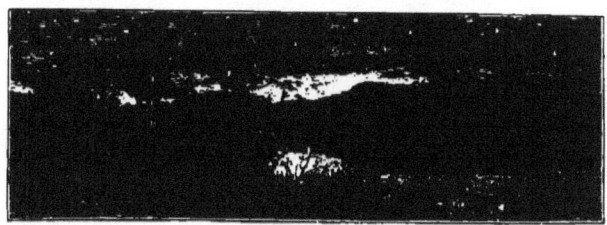

Anon we saw him lounging 'neath the trees,
  Sporting in shady woods and waterfalls,
Fanning himself with every passing breeze,
  And listening the herdsman's cattle-calls,—
Until plump Autumn, bursting with her stores,
  Brought votive offerings to the pursy Year,
And opened wide her golden folding-doors
  To any debauchee in search of cheer.

We saw him enter, and around him sprung
  A hundred nymphs, in beauty's filmiest robes,
Bringing him cups of purple juices wrung
  From out the sweet hearts of the clustering globes,
And loading him with lusciousness, until
  His arms, broad shoulders, back, neck, head, and all
Were one vast mass of mellow fruits;—and still
  (The doors swung to) we did not see him fall!

But when last eve we saw him toiling on,
  And knew his hours were numbered, we went out
And took him by the arm—his strength was gone—
  And sought to lead him to discourse about
The story of his life—a " fourfold tale "—
  But broken words[a] were all that met the ear :
" Starvation "—" floods "—" oppression "—" woe
    and wail "—
    " Scallawags "—" insurrection"—" Ku Klux "—
    " fear " —
" Drought " — " reconstruction " — " constitution
    damned "—
    " The freedmen's bureau "—" earthquakes "—
    " pestilence "—

" Volcanoes " — " robbers " — " ships in icefloes
    jammed "—
    " Collisions "—" carpet-baggers "—" accidents "——

When o'er the sleeping city the great tongue
  Of the cathedral bell struck "One—two—three"
To "twelve"—and then the Old Year lay among
  His myriad brothers that had ceased to be :
The iron hammer which that giant swung
  Had beaten out his life and set him free !

In that weird hour we stood alone,—or thought
  We stood alone,—and heard the mighty wings
Of Father Time, who crumbles worlds to nought,
  Go sweeping by, bearing the shadowy things
Of the dead Past to their eternal home,—
  The chief among them EIGHTEEN SIXTY-EIGHT,—
And with his vast collection, the great tome

That wraps all histories like the Book of Fate :—
And so we said,—" Farewell, thou grand Old Year!
  With all thy faults and follies thou did'st bring
Pleasures and benefits untold—perchance a tear!
  We'll shed a few for thee, thou fallen king!"

A watchman on the Southern walls, we cry,—
  " The day is breaking! rouse ye from your sleep!
The New Year dawns! and up the eastern sky
  The infant prodigy begins to creep!
E'en now from over all the groaning lands
  A thousand voices call, ' What cheer?' ' What cheer?'
And we reply,—Hope, smiling blandly, stands,
  And wears the features of the glad New Year!
Sweet Plenty,—daughter of the fruitful sun,—
  Sits kindly at your boards ; and heavenly Peace,
With all her glowing train, has just begun
  To break your fetters, giving swift release.
Let all the dead Past bury all its dead!
  Look not behind! onward and upward press!
Let the grand Future stand for you in stead
  Of vanished hopes and faded loveliness!
Put your own shoulders to the jaded wheel
  Of the great Car that moves the nations on,
And so, with iron arms and hearts of steel,
  The highest heaven of glory shall be won ;—
Forgetting not allegiance true to give
  To the Great Monarch of the earth and sky,
And to the Commonwealth in which you live,
  And to the Starry Flag that gleams on high!"

53

FROM THE PIAZZA

ACROSS his breast the autumn sunbeams fall,
   While up his shaggy side the shadows creep
From foot to crown,—a flock of mountain sheep
Slow climbing homeward at the shepherd's call,
Scaling with certain foot the jagged wall,
   O'erleaping gulfs and cañons wildly deep
   Within whose cells the storm-winged Furies sleep,—
Until they gather at their starlit stall.
      And up the iron trail the genii go,
         With sturdy shoulders pushing venturous trains,
            While the grim mountain shakes his sides with
            glee
      To see his faithful vassals toiling so.
         At last the clouds engulf them, and it rains :
         So great ships vanish in a thunderous sea.

54

THE PRESIDENTIAL RANGE

THE BOATMAN

ONE autumn day, when all the sweet-voiced woods
Were laughing merrily in their solitudes,
And when the arms of Mother Earth were full
Of fruits delicious, odorous, beautiful,
There floated down the river of my rhyme
A drowsy listener to the far-off chime
Of sweetest bells, that from the hazy shore
The throbbing ether to the Boatman bore.

And while his soul on restless wings was gone,
The silent-sandalled waters drifted on,—
Past stately shores, high crowned with statelier towers,
Where dallying day prolonged the festal hours,—
Past verdurous slopes, whose soft and tempting breast
Sore lured the wanderer to longed-for rest,—
Until, like sapphires in a maiden's dream,
A thousand stars lay flashing in the stream.

And over all,—the slopes, the towers, the hill,
The murmuring water and the Boatman still,—
The stealthy moon her filmy network flung;
But Darkness, terrified, aside had sprung,
And, mounting hastily the tethered breeze,
Fled to his hiding-place among the trees,

57

His hoof-beats pattering on the yellow leaves
Like summer rain-drops from the summer eaves.

Yet still the Boatman floated down the shores ;
His nerveless hands still grasped the nerveless oars,
For o'er the waves came such melodious swells,
That all the air seemed resonant of bells ;—
As on the morning when the earth was young
A universe of worlds their pæan rung ;
Or in some dim, sequestered wood, the birds
Fill all the sounding aisles with liquid words.

The Boatman leaned bewildered on his hand,
For round him floated, beautiful and grand,
Faces and forms he had not seen before,
Steering his shallop to the shelving shore,—
While the mild moon a shadowy Temple threw
Beneath the answering waters, till there grew
Upon his vision scenes of fairy-land,
As lightly shifting as the shifting sand.

They reached the shore—the Boatman and his crew ;—
They led him up the path all gemmed with dew
Which Nature—kindly priestess—had been wont
To scatter from her benedictive font,—
Until they gained the utmost terrace, when
Such floods of glory burst upon his ken,
That speechless, motionless, entranced he stood,
A willing victim for the kindling wood.

THE BOATMAN

Yet flowed the river on—but not for him ;
The shallop beckoned from the water's brim ;
The waves, that erst breathed music in his ear,
Now called in vain—the Boatman could not hear ;—
Nor eye nor ear had he for sight or sound
Save for the fane on that enchanted ground,
Whose vast entablature rode, high and bold,
Nine caryatids of the purest mould.

So Atlas, grimly bending 'neath his load,
Through fields foundationless his pathway strode,
While round and round him sun and moon and stars
Drave their fierce coursers and their fiery cars,
Glad homage paying to the stern intent
Of that unyielding back, yet sorely bent,
Which, all uncheered by hope of victor's crown,
Had never paused to lay its burden down.

And over all the Temple's massive walls,
Its mullioned windows lighting twilight halls,
Its grand entablature, and spires, and dome,
An evergreen of rarest beauty clomb ;
And peering out beneath its sheltering green,
Like Love 'neath lashes of some rustic queen,
The Boatman saw the faces of his dream
While floating idly on the errant stream.

At last they bound him to the crackling pile ;
The glad wild bell pealed joyously the while ;

The blazing fagots waved their lambent flame ;
He heard sweet voices calling him by name ;
The curling smoke with smothering kisses crept
Close to his lips and brow -- the Boatman slept ; --
But when the sunlight on that Temple shone,
It sent back greeting from an added stone.

"As the tall corn parted right and left" —

THE OLD MAN'S "YESTERDAY."

"WAS 'T yesterday? Yes, 't was yesterday!
 It must have been yesterday morn :
I sat on a rock by the River Ray,
 Where the squadrons of martial corn
Their silken banners had just unfurled
 To the breeze, by the singing stream,
When a vision of beauty, all golden-curled,
 Grew into my waking dream.

"I know it was yesterday, for now
 The rustle I seem to hear,
As the tall corn parted right and left,
 And a voice rang soft and clear,—
'Wait, Willie, wait! I am almost there!
 I said I would grant your wish,
So I 've made a line of my golden hair,
 And am coming to help you fish!'

"Yes! (why do I doubt?) it *was* yesterday—
 For I see the soft tassels there
Sunning themselves in a worshipful way
 In the light of her shining hair,
While her voice rings merrily over the corn,—
 'Oh, Willie! come help me through,

63

For I am "the maiden all forlorn,"
    And my feet are wet with dew!

" 'And you know I 'm coming to help you fish :
    But you 'll think me a silly girl,
For I have n't a bit of bait—but wait!
    I 'll bait with a tiny curl!
And, Willie, say, do you think they 'll bite?
    And then what shall I do?
Must I pull and pull with all my might?
    But I 'll wait, and look at you!'

"Ah, me! ah, me! *was* it yesterday?
    It seems but a day ago!
Yet three-score years of yesterdays
    Have covered my head with snow
Since we sat, where the summer still comes and goes,
    I and my sweetheart May,
On the rock where the ripples kissed our toes,
    And fished in the River Ray."

OH! 'T WAS THE FUNNIEST THING

BUT I 'LL TELL YOU ALL ABOUT IT

"I 'D had a d'licious birthday! I was just 'xactly
    eight:
So mamma told my grandpapa, who came in awful late,
Soon after all the dollies and their mothers 'd gone away,
And I and Ann Maria were so tired we *could n't* play,
Although I 'm sure *he* wanted to——but grandpapa is
    nice:
He said he 'd 'xcuse us this time, but he could n't do it
    twice!

"And was n't it the sweetest thing?—dear mamma
    'ranged it all!—
To have my birthday come in May, when apple-blossoms
    fall
Like great warm rosy snow-flakes all over the soft grass,
And the dandelions have to blow and struggle through
    the mass
To get their heads above the snow, p'cisely as the boys
Do in the winter-time, but not with such a mis'ble noise!

" So after dolly 'd said her prayers—I b'lieve I 'd said
    mine too—
And mamma 'd kissed me—just how many times I never
    knew—

65

And said ' Good-night, with pleasant dreams,' and tucked
    us both in tight.
(You wouldn't b'lieve it! but I tumbled out of bed one
    night
And bumped my nose!—'e-'e-'e-'e!) I never knew a
    thing
Until, along towards morning, I heard a ting-a-ling-ling.

" Well, p'r'aps I wasn't wide awake!—but I just gave
    a leap
Right out of bed, and left poor Ann Maria fast asleep,
And hurried to the window where it opens on the lawn—
And what d' you think I saw out there, all in the early
    dawn?
Why, forty hundred dew-bells rung by forty hundred elves!
Nobody heard those elfin chimes but just me—and them-
    selves!

" I heard them ring as plain as day ;—and down among
    the trees
I saw the funniest goings-on!—Some great fat Bumble-
    bees,
And Humming-birds, and Butterflies, and lots of other
    things—
Each one before a dew-drop mirror prinked, and stretched
    her wings,
And combed her hair—then washed her face and bathed
    her pretty toes
In the little pools that nestled in some sleepy Jacquemi-
    nots.

"And then to end their frolic, all their toilets being
  done,
They found a 'normous dew-drop, just as golden as the
  sun,
Almost as fat and jolly, which they whirled and danced
  around—
The skirt dance !—I know how myself !—with not a sin-
  gle sound
Except the cut-glass elfin bells, and the laughter of the
  bees
As they kicked, and bowed, and swayed, and twisted,
  underneath the trees.

" I couldn't stand it 'nother minute—rushed headlong
  down the stair,
Barefooted, in my ' nighty,' dragging dolly by the hair,
My own hair flying wildly, and we joined the merry-go-
  round
Till the dew-drop grew so dizzy she rolled over on the
  ground :
'T was then the Butterfly trod upon old Bumble's sorest
  toe,
And the touchy thing just threatened 'sassination to her
  'foe !

" *She always carried—so she said—a dagger or two for use
In just such cases, and 't would give her pleasure to intr'-
  duce——*
But the speech was never finished, for the Butterfly flew
  away,

And the Bumblebee sent for a doctor, and the rest of us
  would n't stay,
And — what seems *most* inexp-p'cable — my mamma
  ' Good-morning ' said,
And I looked around, and there we were, both snug in
  our little bed !''

—"your doom
is whispered down the grim and silent halls."

THE PRINCES IN THE TOWER

YOU wander hand in hand from room to room—
  On every side barred windows and dead walls ;
Dark shadows lurk in corners, and your doom
  Is whispered down the grim and silent halls.
Go to your couch, my Princes ! Let the sleep
  Of sweet forgetfulness sit on your eyes
And dull your ears : so may your dreams be deep
  The while you pass unconscious to the skies.

      But that was O so long ago !
        The princes of to-day
      Are free as birds to come and go
        From morn till evening gray.
      They are not smothered, drowned, or burned—
        Their feet are fleet as wings :
      Before we know it, they are turned
        From princes into kings.

71

O GEMINI

A PRECIOUS pair of rascals, truly !
    Up to all sorts of pranks unruly !
Fun and frolic in every motion !
As many moods as the changeful ocean—
    Sunshine and tempest any day !
What has become of the household quiet ?
Gone !—and ducats could n't buy it !
    Where did you come from, any way ?

Does Leda know you have gone a-Maying—
Gone, from the fields of gold a-straying ?
Did the watchful hosts of heaven say things
When you threw away your starry playthings ?
    How they must miss you ilka day !
And such a long, dark journey—sleepy,
And all alone, and hungry, weepy !—
    You must have come by the Milky Way.

The world is brighter since you love us ;
But the fields of gold are dark above us,
For now, at night, when you are calling,
The glist'ning stars, like tears, are falling—

72

O GEMINI

Falling for their lost Gemini :
But though the weeping heavens miss you,
And Leda longs to hug and kiss you,
    We cannot spare you—Clem and I.

73

THE ROAD AND THE RIVER

IT was an eerie Road, but beautiful—in places :
  It wound along the foot of wooded hills,
Now underneath great beetling cliffs with sullen faces,
  Then down the softest valleys where the trills
Of sylvan songsters filled the laughing, flower-clad
   meadows
  With music till the hour of evening prayer :
Then picked its way through undiscovered, starlit
   shadows,
  To places slumberful, and strange to care.

The Road was wide and long—it had no known begin-
   ning ;
  The end no mortal eye would ever see :—
Forms tantalizing, beautiful, well worth the winning,
  Seemed ever beck'ning to some Good to be.
And so the Road wound in and out—across morasses
  That shook beneath the tramp of host on host,
While up and down and through the darkened mountain
   passes
  The tireless way led on from post to post.

Beside this antique Road, unseen, unheard, a River
  Forever hugged the shore ;—its stealthy tread—

So soft and velvety it was—ne'er caused a shiver
   Among the heedless throng, nor thought of dread.
They could not hear the dip of oars, nor yet the singing
   The fragrant air across the River bore ;
They could not hear the eager swish of angels winging
   Their joyful errands on the sunlit shore.

The River was not always deep, for sparkling shallows
   Made music, sometimes, for the children's ears ;
Sometimes a glimpse across to where the sweet marsh-
      mallows
   Were growing, filled their wistful eyes with tears ;
And once a little one, the darling of her mother,
   Her bare toes gleaming on the shining sand,
And, closely guarding her, her watchful, brown-eyed
      brother,
   Went wading through the ripples hand in hand—

And they were seen no more, their sunny faces hidden
   By floods of mist, perchance by floods of tears.
But no one left that dusty, crowded Road unbidden :
   I watched them closely through the maze of years,
And always—somehow, somewhere, sometime—still, un-
      sleeping—
   The voiceless boatman of the silent sea
Was waiting at the brink, unmindful of the weeping,
   To row the traveller to the far countree.

A PORTRAIT FROM THE SEA

STRANGE Slavic face!—I mind the morning well
    When first I met you on that pebbly shore!
Old Ocean steadfastly refused to tell
How he had polished you with every swell
    For ages; how he rolled you o'er and o'er
    The threshold of the beach's open door,
A clear-cut portrait (artist, Wind-and-Wave),
A foundling rescued from a watery grave.
    I wonder if St. Vladimir the Great
    E'er used your droshky in his rides of state!
Or did the face you counterfeit so well
Look last on earth from some foul prison cell?
    Not tell the secret of your age or birth!
    Why, fur-capped Russian! what's your secret worth?

"Putting to soft Cistern, in dreary mist."

ON THE ROCKS AT YORK

AHA, old Ocean!—so I find you here,
  Just as I left you years and years ago,
Unruffled, beautiful, a world of blue,—
  To-morrow, doubtless, to be decked with snow
In dancing drifts upon an azure field,
  While o'er your face the warm south breezes blow.

A calm, inviting, gently rippling sea,
  Your clear-cut facets flashing in the sun,
Purring in soft content, in sleepy ease,
  After the frolics of the day are done,
Whispering wild legends to the bearded rocks
  Ere yet the moon her journey has begun.

Oft have I seen you kiss their rugged lips,
  Pledge them eternal fealty and trust,
Lull them to confidence with siren song,
  And then, upon the first great windy gust,
Fly at their faces, shrieking loud and long,
  Doing your best to grind them into dust.

" Thus far "—" no farther " (?)—See the rocky shore
  Slowly recede before the blows that fall
From that old giant Tide-and-Wind-and-Wave !

79

On all tempestuous nights I hear him call,—
And night-fiends come, with battle-axe and ram,
And thunder at the gray and crumbling wall.

And so, old Sea, you eat the shore away:
The æons pass—the mountains fill the sea,
Gnawed into fragments by the tooth of Time:
Some day, some day—it matters not to me—
The continent will vanish, as this rhyme,
And sea and sunset clasp their hands in glee.

SILVER WEDDING BELLS

"BETTER fifty years of Europe than a cycle of
Cathay,"
Sang a poet of our Fatherland, three thousand miles
away,—
On a little sea-girt island, just the bigness of your hand,
Which the waves will wash away, some day, like piles
of silver sand.

But by "Europe" he meant England, as his rhythmic
numbers rolled :
All the world beyond the Channel had been left out in
the cold.
Pity overspread his features, with contempt not far away,
As he thought of England's glory—and the wretches of
Cathay !

"How they envy us our good things ! How they long to
come in flocks
To this island," thought the poet, "where we live like
fighting cocks !
Where the blessed sun shines every day—beyond the
clouds and fogs !
And where no blarsted Frenchman lives to gobble up
our frogs !"

With sentiments akin to these, the happy pair to-night
Look down upon the common world, from off the dizzy
    height
Toward which, for just one hundred years—less seventy
    and five!
They 've bravely climbed, through sun and storm, and
    wonder they 're alive!

" ' Survival of the fittest!'—look at us and see how true!
Those who reach this sun-crowned pinnacle are really
    very few!
And then, to think what we have done!—look round
    upon our sons!
Four stalwart boys, as brave as ever fired their country's
    guns!

" How many have done better? Count your jewels o'er
    and o'er,
And if, perchance, in counting them you make the
    number more,
Thank Him who made your cup of life's rich juices
    overflow
In sweeter draughts of happiness than angels ever
    know!

" With deep and true thanksgiving, and with placid
    souls to-night,
We gaze upon the faded years, so rapid in their flight,
With a sort of mellow pity for the men and maidens fair
Who here have shut out heaven, while not certain of it
    there!' "

Such are the pleasing fancies that go coursing through
the brains
Of host and hostess, like the steeds of Arabs o'er the
plains :
We will not grudge them one bright thought, for ne'er
for them on earth
Will such a morning dawn again, or such a day have
birth.

———

I remember well the morning, although 't was long ago !
Jack Frost had limned the window-panes—outside, the
creaking snow :
The lazy sun lay shivering in bed behind the hills :
He had no wife to keep him warm—the worst of human ills !

He drew the blankets tightly round his head and lusty
form,
For 't was a morning when a bed of coals could not
keep warm :
The breakfast bell he scouted, his hair was all un-
kempt,
And for weddings he professed to feel the most sublime
contempt.

Such was the situation ;—in a room not far away—
I see it now as plainly as though 't were yesterday—
Warm friends and kindly neighbors had gathered one
by one
To say " God-speed," and kiss the bride—a jewel fairly
won.

They stood before the minister, this young and lovely
  pair,—
He young—she lovely—both young : I am bound to
  treat them fair !
Brave words were softly said—a maiden vanished like
  the dew :
That moment — — — — disappeared from mortal view.

Ends the story. They are with us ;—five-and-twenty
  years ago
They began their pleasant journey, when the world was
  dressed in snow,
Robed expressly for the wedding, robed in white again
  to-night,
While the moon, true love's assistant, sheds o'er all her
  tender light.

Blessings on them—blessings ever ! May their last years
  be their best !
May they gaze with tranquil rapture toward the gateway
  of the west,
Where all things bright and beautiful—the sun, the
  moon, the stars—
In long processions disappear behind the golden bars.

THE NORTH WIND'S WINTER OUTING

BOLD Buccaneer! from your starry tent,
    Where the frost king cannot bind you,
You scurry away, on mischief bent,
    With your crew of howls behind you :
Ride fast and far, till your horses' neigh
    And the clang of your spurs and lances
Are heard from the close to the break of day
    In the children's dreamland fancies.
            Blow-w-w !   Blow-w-w !

Drive headlong down great Baffin bay,
    Plough deep the cringing water,
Till the thousand storm-born Furies play
    At the game of wreck and slaughter :
Fly thundering down the slopes of snow
    On your plunging ice toboggan,
Your war-cry heard by friend and foe —
    The North Wind's mighty slogan !
            Blow-w-w !   Blow-w-w !

Shriek madly—howl to your heart's content,
    Demoniac wind of the winter !
Blow high ! blow low ! till your strength is spent —
    The strength of an Arctic sprinter !

Go trumpeting through the mountain woods
  Like a giant Son of Thunder,
And waken the torpid solitudes
  As the hemlocks split asunder.
      Blow-w-w! Blow-w-w!

Seize hold of the elm trees' shivering limbs,
  And give the old roof a lashing
To the tune of your ringing battle hymns
  And the toppling tiles down-crashing :
Push recklessly through that clapboard rent
  Where the out- with the inside mingles,
And, to give our spirits a freer vent,
  Take a twist at the mossy shingles.
      Blow-w-w! Blow-w-w!

You have wrecked fair ships and have played
    with Death,
  Fierce foe of the icebound seaman!
Have shaken our cot with your gusty breath
  The breath of a storm-brewed demon!

But come to the door by the frosty path
　　And list to the children's prattle,
The crackling logs on the blazing hearth,
　　And the teakettle's tittle-tattle.
　　　　Blow-w-w! Blow-w-w!

The children play where the firelight falls—
　　Outside, the snow is flying!
The shadows dance on the laughing walls—
　　Who cares for the North Wind's sighing!
Go back, wild tramp, bewildered, dumb,
　　To your home where the mercury freezes;
But come again when the blue-birds come,
　　In the softest of vernal breezes.
　　　　Blow-w-w! Blow-w-w!

Yᴱ BALADE OF Yᴱ FRETFULL LYTEL ROBIN

BLASING sumer afternone :—
No breth of aire was steringe ;
Yᵉ frogges blynked 'neath yᵉ lilie-paddles ;
No partriches were whurring.

Yᵉ grases wulde nott bend their heds,
Nor whysper to eche other ;
Yᵉ lambs, in lamb's-wooll sumer suites,
Were sure that they sholde smother.

Yᵉ kow stood kne-deepe in yᵉ pool
Where temptinge schade hadde broghte hir :
Hir nerveless taille hung limpe and stille
Above yᵉ steaminge water.

Yᵉ bumblenbees, on languid winges,
Went hom, and ceased their humming,
And in their easy-chaires they dremed
Of cool Septembre's coming.

Yᵉ molten sunne runne downe yᵉ west,
Impacient for yᵉ shelter
Beyond yᵉ cool grene mountain-toppes—
Yᵉ daye was suche a melter !

90

A panting lytel Robin, perched
  Amonge y͏ͤ rede-cheeked cheries,
So overcome hee coude nott pyke
  Y͏ͤ tantalising beries,—

Schokk͏ᵈ his mamma with dreadfull wordes :
  " If thys͏ˢ y͏ͤ kinde of wether
You ͏ᵛᵉ hatched mee to, I wisch—I wisch—
  I ͏ᵈᵈᵉ nott a single fether

" Upon my bak—so there !"—Atte thys
  Y͏ͤ precious lytel mother
Just gasped—and sobbed ;—shee coude nott chide
  Thys childe—shee hadde no other.

But whenne y͏ͤ father homeward came
  Acros y͏ͤ feeldes of clover,
And herde y͏ͤ sad, sad storie, thenne
  Hee sente a lettre over

To Robin-toun for twenty byrdes
  To sitte in consultation
Upon thys case of mutinie
  Within y͏ͤ Robin nation.

They sate within y͏ͤ cherie-tree—
  Eche Robin took a cherie—
Whiles on a distant lim y͏ͤ childe
  Of sinne sate solemne—very.

Y^e final verdit was, that eche
And everie single fether
Sholde bee pulled off ye Robin's bak,
Regardless of ye wether,—

And that hee thenne bee turned aloofe
To rome ye wyde worlde over,
A hatteless, coteless, homless byrde,
Without a frend or lover.

Atte once they fell upon ye childe—
Thys sterne, relentless jurie—
And wulde have torn eche fether out
In their ungoverned furie,—

Hadde nott ye farmer's trustie gunne
Just thenne begunne its cracking:
In fiftene minutes twenty byrdes
In Robin-land were lacking.

Nexte daye ye morn was cool and bright:
Y^e farmer hadde for dinner
A most delicious Robin-pye:
A sweete songe sang ye sinner

Oute in ye orcherd where ye breese
Swung high ye mocking beries,
And filled his downie basket fulle
Of rype, rede-brested cheries.

HOW CAN YOU EVER FIND ME

"IT is so hard, my love, my more than life,
　　To say Good-bye ;
To leave the arms so empty, where your wife
　　Found it so sweet to lie ;
No kisses—oh ! it cuts me like a knife,
　　Dear one, just to lie down and die,
E'en though your great heart guards my slumber deep,
　　And June's warm tones, in whispers low,
Break lovingly upon my dreamless sleep,
　　And I can hear you go,
And come again, and go, and hear you weep,
　　You love me so.

" And, dearest, when you come to that far land
　　Where I shall be,
I may not know the place upon the strand
　　Of the deep crystal sea
Where your light boat will touch ;—I may not stand
　　With outstretched arms, where you can see
The face you long for ;—I may be away
　　On some most sweet and holy quest :—
How can you ever find me, then ?—the way
　　Will seem so long, at best,
Till your dear head may lie again, some day,
　　Upon my breast."

93

" Dear heart, it will be easy, when I go,
    To find you there,
For all the heavenly throng will surely know
    Your dazzling, sunlit hair,
So radiantly beautiful, and so
    Will make sweet haste to tell me where
My hungry heart may find you—in what realm
    Of beauty. I shall listen long,
Beneath the shade of some o'erarching elm,
    For snatches of a song
That will my soul with rapture overwhelm
    And make me strong.

" And I shall follow it—no song so sweet
    Was ever heard ;
Shall wildly listen for your footsteps fleet,
    Swifter than any bird :—
And when the violets beneath your feet
    Breathe in your breath, their fragrance stirred
By your glad coming ; and the ruddy gleams
    Of parted lips, just touched with dew,
Break through the trees : and the warm, limpid beams
    Of loving eyes of blue
Come flying to my arms—Good-bye, wild dreams !
    I shall have you."

"The orchard young globes

FAIR ORMOND

FAIR Ormond of the sunbright shore —
    How sweet our memories be !
The restful river at her door ;
    Behind, the white-fringed sea.

The wild waves chant her sweetest charms—
    She turns her face away !
The warm breeze clasps her in his arms
    And kisses her all day.

A Queen, no jewelled robe she lacks :
    She reigns right royally,
One soft hand on the Halifax,
    The other on the sea.

Her orange groves are wondrous fair :
    The clustered yellow globes
Are grouped in constellations there—
    Thrown back their royal robes

Of emerald-green, so longing eyes
    May feast on golden worlds

That hang for aye in Southern skies
 For orange-blossom girls.

The live-oaks swing the woodland sprites
 In loops of ashen gray,
When lovers crowd the moonlight nights,
 And fairy-land is gay.

Through massive golden sunset bars
 The day departs in state,
While one by one the wizard stars
 Steal through the twilight gate

To gaze on bloody fields of old,
 Of Spanish derring-do,

98

Where Ponce de Leon fought for gold
　And Indian arrows flew.

And if we listen when the doors
　Of night are all ajar,
The rhythmic dip of shadowy oars
　Will greet us from afar.

Where scintillant Tomoka glides,
　With heaven above, below,
Red warriors wooed their wild-rose brides :
　And still his waters flow

As calmly, mutely to the sea
　As ever waters ran,—
The loveliest dream in Florida,
　An Arcady for Pan.

Fair Ormond ! you are wondrous sweet—
    Your flowers, your birds, your trees ;—
We kiss again your dainty feet :
    We feel your cooling breeze.

ANNIVERSARY POEM [5]

IN a far Eastern land—the splendid Sunrise Land—
  There lived a king, three thousand years ago :
So wise was he, so gentle, and so large of heart,
  That all the kings of earth would come, and go,
And come again, to question him, and catch the pearls
  Of wisdom that, like gleaming drops of dew,
Fell from his rich, ripe lips. His fame spread over all
  The lands ; and once a queen, with retinue
Of camels that bore spices, and much gold, and stones
  Most precious—the most beautiful and wise
Of women—came to prove him with hard questionings.
  The half had not been told ;—she veiled her eyes ;
There was no spirit left in her. She sadly turned—
  This proud and noble dame—back to her own
Fair land, with all her train of servants, cattle, gifts,
  And stores of wisdom hitherto unknown,
A nobler, sweeter, purer, queenlier queen
Than wise King Solomon had ever seen.

But once—so runs the tale—the great King Solomon
  Received command from a far Greater King
To build a palace—a grand temple—to His Name,
  Whose richness and magnificence should ring

Adown the vibrant ages—unapproachable
    By king or potentate, ere yet the tide
Of time should drift us all upon the farther shore
    And close the record on the hither side.

The great king called his builders and his architects
    Into close counsel, and his plans were told:
But there were not, in all his realm, artificers
    In wood and brass and ivory and gold
With skill and subtle wisdom equal to the task
    Of inlaid work and carvèd cherubim,
Gigantic pillars of bright brass, a molten sea
    With just three hundred knops beneath the brim,
And lions, massive oxen, brazen wheels, and all
    The thousand other weird and wondrous things
That made this palace of the Greater King divine—
    A Wonder of the World, as history sings.

The great king's heart was sorely troubled, and he went
    To the high tower where he was wont to pray,
And drew a soft divan to the great window, where
    He could o'erlook the city ;—'t was broad day—
But he was weary, sad, and sick at heart, for he
    Could see no sunshine brightening his way.
Some unseen finger touched his tremulous eyes—he
        slept.
    A voice familiar fell upon his ear:
"O king! take heart of grace: thy father's dearest
        friend,
    The king of Tyre, will help thee: never fear!

Awake! e'en now his servant standeth at thy door
  With kindly messages for David's son."
The king awoke: the dream was true—the problem
    solved:
  The dreamer's face shone like the rising sun.

Meanwhile (the king was very near the hearts of all
  His loyal subjects) a vague rumor spread
Throughout the city that his heart was troubled sore
  Because he had no artisan with head
Sufficient for the royal task; and sympathy
  And tender helpfulness and kindly words
Came up from every side. But one bright early morn
  A flock of brilliant plumaged, white-winged birds
Came flying o'er the city from the smiling west,
  And all the air was full of sparkling song.
Which seemed to say to all those eager ears,—"Cheer
    up,
  For help is coming, and 't will not be long!
Look to the west! Cheer up!"—and then they circled
    round
  And o'er the expectant city, till the hearts
Of all grew lighter than the lightest thistle-down:
  E'en merchants came from all the crowded marts
To join the throng: and as they gazed, came winding
    down
  The hills, with rapid, graceful, easy swing,
A long procession—horses, camels, men—and at
  Their head the grand old man from Tyre—the king!

As this great retinue approached the wide-eyed throng,
  And recognition came like lightning flash—
" Hiram of Tyre!" they cried—" The king! Hiram the
    king!
    Hiram our benefactor!" Crash on crash
The shouts rolled back in thunder peals, wave after
    wave,
  Over the city, over vale and hill,
Dying away in faintest echoes, as dies the storm
  At the great Master's mandate, "Peace! be still!"

So Solomon and Hiram, friends and lovers, built
  That wondrous pile. Their fleets sailed side by side
To Ophir, and brought back great store of ivory,
  And gold, and precious stones, and fabrics dyed
In the rich colors of those dim, barbaric climes,
  To decorate the temple. And the king
Of Tyre denuded Lebanon of cedars, firs,
  And everything of worth, that he might bring
The oil of gladness to its humble worshippers.
  And when the task of that seven years was done—
The twice one hundred thousand artisans at rest—
  That regal dream stood flashing in the sun,
The grandest epic of the ages, and the best.

So runs the strange old story ;—it is quaintly told
  On dim and musty parchments, in the deep
And dark recesses of an ancient monastery
  In the far East, where strangest legends sleep,

And only curious travellers, who dig and delve
    For hidden gems, can rouse them from their slumbers :
Let them sleep.

Alas for that grand pile !   Where, where is it to-day ?
    No eye for five-and-twenty hundred years
Has gazed upon its towers and peerless pinnacles :
    'T is buried in a soundless sea of tears.

———

Another temple, not so grand and beautiful,
    We sing to-day ; a temple reared by hands
And hearts and brains as true as ever struck a blow
    For love of God and man in Eastern lands :
A temple round whose modest pillars cling the loves
    Of thousands who have worshipped at its shrine,
Whose tender memories, quivering through the haze of
        years,
    Dress it in robes that seem almost divine :
A temple reared to Education, Truth, and God,
    Most of whose builders lie beneath the sod.

And yet this temple groweth still—it is not done :
    Of years three score and ten and five, it stands
Baring its white, cool, youthful forehead to the sun,
    Gazing adown the centuries, its hands
Outstretched in passionate welcome to the splendid sons
    And daughters of the future, whose clear eyes—
As full of sweetest laughter as your mountain brooks—
    Shall aye reflect the nations' destinies.

Here shall they come, in troops, to taste the cooling
   spring,
And thirsty souls shall drink, and drink again,
And, passing out these academic doors, shall go
   To lift to higher planes their fellow-men.

Another Hiram,[6] too, we sing, and every inch
   A man, a king,—yea, every inch a king
No whit the less than he of fragrant memory
   Whose praise the Poet has essayed to sing.
The strength and wisdom of his ripe and golden years,
   His forceful guiding hand and teeming brain,
Helped fashion here a fane so grand, we could but think
   The king of Tyre had come to earth again.

To-day we saw a long procession winding up
   The hill, in gay attire, and at its head
A form and face familiar in the years gone by :
   Our hearts were lighter, baleful fancies fled,
For in that noble form we saw Hiram the king !
   And warm hearts greeted him with silent cheers.
No crown of gold sat heavy on his brow—instead,
   The rime of wisdom and of four-score years,
As light and airy as the fleecy clouds of June
   Afloat in ether,—and an easy grace,
Born of a life well spent, spread o'er his countenance :
   We thought he had a wondrous lovely face.
Welcome, King Hiram, to your own !—a kingdom won
By the sheer force of duties nobly, grandly done !

And here, upon the summit of this sun-crowned height,
  A beacon light, this modern temple stands,
And hearts of gold will turn to her their eager feet,
  Drawn to her altars by her high commands.
Her gracious light shall not be hid ;—like Joseph's kin,
  The sun, the moon, and the eleven stars,
And all the circling mountains, feel their pulses thrill
  With humble homage, and shall leap the bars
That stand between them and old Thetford Hill.

The Poet, from the vantage-ground of his high tower
  Upon the rocky, thunderous coast of Maine,
Looks out of his wide window on the turbulent sea
  And sees uncounted ships, an endless train,
Go sailing by, and every canvas swelling with
  The hope and faith that high endeavor knows.
How eagerly the white arms welcome every breeze
  From softest kisses to the hardest blows !
See how the salt spray leaps and flashes in the sun,
  And falls in cooling drops upon the prow !
See how the dancing waters humbly step aside
  To leave a pathway for the gleaming plow !
And you can hear the jocund voices of the crew
  Come lilting o'er the waves—I hear them now !
So each fair ship goes sailing on, and on, and
  on,
  Bound to some far-off port—God only knows
The where, or whether its great anchor ever will
  Be cast where never more the wild wind blows ;

Or whether, as the full ripe years go marching by,
  These brave craft, weather-beaten, canvas-torn,
Will proudly sail across the harbor bar of home
  And cast their anchors where their hopes were born.

Old Thetford Hill has sent her noblest craft to sea:
  Where are they now?—Sometimes she cries, with
    tears,
" When will my ships—my splendid ships—come back
  to me?
  When will my ships come home?" But darkest fears
Give place to triumph! Look! This early morn a soft
  Brisk breeze across the white-capped waters blew;
A fleet of bellying sail came flying down the wind,
  On every deck a bronzed, stout-hearted crew;—
And look around you now! These faces—do you know?—
Are but the ships old Thetford launched—her ships of
  Long Ago.

"R___v__d i__ mod__t t_st_ 't now."

TWO APPLES[7]

EVE

BEAUTIFUL, Queen of the shadowy aisles,
  Lighting their depths with your innocent wiles!
    Wander not far from the whispering tree :
    Adam lies under it dreaming of thee.
Doubt is already disturbing his rest :
Golden head! go back and lie on his breast.

Empress of Hearts the world over, beware!
Dangers beset thee, so young and so fair ;—
    Touch not the rosy-red fruit on the bough :
    Rosy-red lips must not taste of it now.

    !   !   !   !   !   !

Eve! O sweet Mother! the world is in tears :
Yet Hope floats serene down the river of years.

TELL.

That massive tree is not more firm of foot
        Than thou art, little Tell !
Thy father planted thee : thou must stay put—
        The why, thou knowest well.
The tree and thou art back to back—stand firm !
        The apple on thy head
Has an uncertain, doubtful footing ;—squirm,
        And off it rolls, like lead !
Cling to the tree !   Steady !   Keep open eyes !
        When all is done, shout "Ready !"
Whiz-z-z !—How that arrow from the stout bow flies !
        Thud !—What, done already ?

THE GARDENS OF NODDY

DOWN in the Gardens of Nid-nod-Noddy,
   Whither my pretty baby 's going,
Nicest things and sweetest things for every baby body
   Are growing—growing——growing.
Little white pearls, like peas in a poddy,
   Out through the rosy gates are peeping,
Down in the Gardens of Nid-nod-Noddy,
   Where my baby 's creeping.

Still are the Gardens of Noddy, and shady—
   None can be warmer or lighter :
Mamma is the sunlight and starlight, the lady
   That makes the gardens sweeter and brighter
For every little baby boy and every little maidy
   That listens to the song she is humming
Down in the gardens where the birdies keep shady,—
   " Nid-nod-Noddy 's coming !"

Daffodils and poppies, hollyhocks and clover,
   Down in the Gardens of Noddy,
Nod their pretty sleepy heads, over and over,
   To every little sleepy-headed body

That wanders through those dreamy aisles to find a cosy
  cover
  Where the Nodheads in their hammocks are swing-
  ing ;
Where are buttercups and daisies, golden-rod and clover,
  Sleepily—sleepily——singing.

Bees are stealing honey, and all about us flying,
  Looking for my pretty darling, maybe,
But if in mamma's drowsy lap they find him snugly
  lying,
  They 'll dare not kiss my blue-eyed little baby.
In the Noddy gardens all the sights and sounds are
  dying—
  Mamma's loving eyes have ceased their beaming ;
All the world has drifted off, like summer clouds a-flying—
  Baby 's dreaming—dreaming.

PARALLELS

INVISIBLE To-morrows crowd the encircling ether!
  The granary of Time is full of them. And when
The great black iron midnight gate falls prone before
  The mighty blows of the cathedral bell, a germ
Shoots forth from its unseen retreat—a burning star
  From darkest background—and the bright To-day is
    born.
So unborn souls are waiting—the uncounted millions
  Of God's sweet thoughts, stored in the vaulted cham-
    bers of
Eternity—for the great summons. One by one,
  Like rain-drops from a balmy summer sky, they come
Out of the vast unseen into the blazing light:
  Birth is their starting-place, and life their grand To-
    day.

To-day sits on the breezy summer hill-tops, smiling;—
  The pliant sun bounds up the cliffs at his command;
He paints fantastic ships upon the bright blue sea
  Above him: bids the song-birds sing, the children play,
And all the world be glad. But Night, remorseless, comes
  And snuffs his candle out: alas! To-day is done!

And Man, whose day began so blithely in the morning
    With touch of mother lips, the robin's song among
The tree-tops, and the sweet breath of the western wind,
    Springs lightly to the helm of his fair ship, and sails
Away into the beck'ning west, a phantom barque.
        Ah me! Night cometh all too soon : his Day is done !

All the To-morrows and To-days since Time came flying
    Across abysmal space, sink in the pulseless sea
Of Yesterdays ;—and Man—immortal, God-like Man—
    Goes with them,—but to rise to a more perfect day
On some bright shore where Death is but a memory,
    And Night is buried in a living sea of Light.

A HUNDRED YEARS AGO [1]

A THOUSAND hearts are swelling
　　With gratitude to-day,
For here, to this His dwelling,
　　Our Saviour leads the way :
We turn the ancient pages,
　　We scan the yellow leaves,
Where Jesus, through the ages,
　　Has written of His sheaves.

We 've heard the simple story
　　Of that courageous band,
The young, and heads all hoary,
　　That came to this fair land,
The pathless wilds before them,
　　The sleepless stars above,
With Heaven bending o'er them,
　　Its great heart full of love.

The dews of June [0] were glist'ning
　　Among the tree-tops there,
And softest breezes list'ning
　　To sadly cadenced prayer,
When on that Sabbath morning
　　A fire began to glow,—

This Church's faint, sweet dawning,
  A hundred years ago.

A hundred years!—How glorious
  Their voices, and how strong,
As down the years, victorious,
  The echoes roll along.
O Christ! like them undaunted
  When overwhelmed with woe,
Come bless the Church they planted
  A hundred years ago.

Now flying wildly through the air to the mill

THE FARM-HOUSE

THE laughing sunshine peers above the hill,
   And down the slumbering vale ;
Then hastens on with nimble feet, until,
A rood or two beyond the silvery rill
Now flying wildly through the ghostly mill,
   He gains the cottage pale.

The hospitable gate stands open wide,
   And, with impatient lips,
The morning-glory beckons to her side
The wayward youth whose quest she ne'er denied ;
Her tangled tresses quick he thrusts aside,
   And dewy nectar sips.

He lingers lovingly among the flowers
   That fringe the open door ;
Then steals within, and wakes with magic powers
The forms at rest in Dreamland's rustic bowers,
And plays through morning's golden-tinted hours
   Upon the oaken floor.

Meanwhile the swirling, effervescent brook
   Halts, and with dainty poise
Leaps headlong to the sparkling, darkling nook,
Where coiled it lies, a-dreaming of the spook,—
The wheezy wheel, that groaned and stretched and shook
   With harsh, blood-curdling noise.

The birds troll welcome to the summer days
   From airy turrets high ;
The bees are humming over ancient lays
That erst were heard in Eden's shaded ways
On that bright morn when universal praise
   Rolled through the arching sky.

Bold chanticleers, with summons loud and shrill,
   The languid echoes wake,
Which just before were sleeping, calm and still,
Behind the pine-coned, breezy, whispering hill
That drinks the cup of morning to its fill,
   Beyond the lazy lake.

The butterflies have stretched their painted wings
   Upon the breath of dawn,
And flit from flower to flower like human things ;
The slaughtered hay its dying perfume flings
Abroad upon the white-winged gale, which brings
   And strews it o'er the lawn.

Beneath the moss-grown roof a group prepare
   To siege the smoking board,
Which fills with grateful incense all the air ;
But first the reverend sire with frosty hair
Craves " daily bread " for those assembled there,
   From Him for aye adored.

Quick follow then the clangings of the steel—
   Above no weltering foe ;
No timid suppliants for mercy kneel,

THE FARM-HOUSE

No vizored foemen with dim vision reel,
But happy voices grace the morning meal
  With love's sweet overflow.

And then the cheerful group contrive to share
  The labors of the day ;
While I, with angling gear and eager air,
Retreat, like lion to his forest lair,
To shady woods where winding streams repair,
  And wile the hours away.

WHERE ROSES GROW

DEAR Land of Love! Sweet Land of Rest!
    We send our loved one home to thee:
Oh! let her lie upon thy breast,
    Soothed by heaven's matchless minstrelsy.

The gates of pearl were opened wide
    To let the wanderer in,
Where peace and rest and joy abide
    With those who dwell therein,—
And we could fancy that we heard
    The angels from afar
Shout Welcome! While a snow-white bird
    Flashed through the gates ajar,
Adown the pathway of the spheres,—
    And our too eager eyes
Could scarcely see, through blinding tears,
    This envoy from the skies.

But messages of love he brought:
    And now we surely know
Those calm blue eyes are fixed upon
    The One who loved her so.

WHERE ROSES GROW

Her tired feet, now tired no more,
  Are strolling by the river
On whose soft banks the roses grow
  And lilies bloom forever.

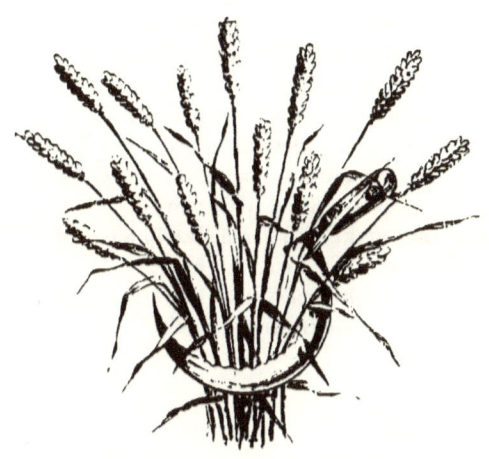

A LAST VISIT

THE dear old trees are just the same ;
   The birds—I know them all ;
The warm winds leap the pine-clad hills
   Responsive to my call,
And kiss me soft on either cheek
   As oft they did of yore :
Alas ! no eager footsteps crowd
   The old familiar door.

The rooms are empty—not a word
   Of welcome greets my ears ;
Their echoes are a mockery—
   My eyes are filled with tears.
I cannot make you seem like home :
   So now, old house, farewell !
Good-bye, old trees, my childhood's friends !
   Good-bye the dear old well !

MARGUERITE

MARGUERITE

BELLE Marguerite ;—the thousand nameless graces
    Of all the queens of beauty
        Since time begun—
The witcheries of all the wondrous faces,
    And voices low and fluty—
        Moulded in one !

Just see her waiting there, the peerless creature !
    The perfect, matchless woman !
        And watch her face :—
Instinct with youth and love is every feature,
    And passionately human
        Is every grace.

Could we but peer behind the filmy laces
    That guard the sweet enclosure
        Where dear Love lies,
A happy bird would smile up in our faces—
    No fear of cold exposure
        Within his eyes.

No queen of hearts was ever half so gracious :
    The apple-blossoms tremble
        With sheer delight

As they stoop down and kiss, with lips audacious,
　That exquisite *ensemble*
　　In pink and white.

The sun's warm fingers, dallying with her tresses,
　Are hopelessly entangled
　　In golden strands :
Nor can he ever set, howe'er time presses,
　Till they are disentangled
　　By loving hands :

Then when the waves of glory round her falling
　Within her vestal chamber
　　Are shut from sight,
If you but listen you may hear him calling
　From off his bed of amber,
　　" Sweet Love !　Good-night ! "

THE LIFE-STREAM

ONE April morning, when the spring
  Released the mountain rill,
I heard the baffled winter wind
  Retreat along the hill.

The father-sun came bending o'er,
  And tenderly caressed
The laughing prattler, as he drew
  His mountain-mother's breast.
The rill, when tired of revelling
  Among the fountains full,
Ran sparkling down the velvet slope
  To sleep—a shady pool.

But when, as morning dawned again,
  He peeped the margin o'er,
And saw the beck'ning buttercups
  Fast marching on before,—
He could not stay; he turned and kissed
  His sleeping mother, then
Stole softly 'neath the lintel green
  And rippled down the glen.

133

As childhood, in uneasy dreams,
   Flies through the green aisles dim
Of some old crooning forest where
   Lurk monsters fierce and grim,—
So fled he, as the stealthy roots
   Of gnarled and wrinkled trees
Came twisting out the loamy bank
   His truant foot to seize.

In most fantastic windings lost,
   In meadows dewy sweet,
To catch the jocund birds that flung
   Their music at his feet,—
He wandered dreamily along
   Till day began to wane,
And sighed, "Ah, me! I ne'er shall see
   My mountain home again."

He hurried down a rocky steep,
   A wild and reckless stream,
And lay all quivering at its foot,
   At rest—perchance to dream
Of that long way he needs must wend,
   The victories to be won,
The blessings waiting at the end
   When all his work was done.

Day after day he travelled on,—
   Grew broad, and deep, and strong,

And turned the ponderous wheels of life
  To rhythmic flow of song.
And while in all the strife of years
  He aimed to bear a part,
A white swan lay upon his breast,
  Her image in his heart.

One hazy autumn afternoon
  The traveller neared the goal
With hurried step and lab'ring breath :
  He heard the thunder roll,
But pressed right onward to the brink,
  Nor shunned the dread abyss,—
His hopes all fixed on realms above,
  One last fond look on this.

Oh ! transformation wonderful !
  Above that gulf, at even,
Hovered a misty form of grace,
  Robed in the hues of heaven !

SPIRIT OF LOVE.[10]

SPIRIT of Love ! touch the eyes that are weeping :
Sweet is her rest who is peacefully sleeping.
Comfort the sorrowing : Hope never dies,
Though love-light be banished from love-lighted eyes :
And sometimes, in the dusk, from the far-brooding dome,
Soft winds will whisper a message from home.
    Lover and Helper ! give them sweet home-rest :
    Pillow their heads on Thy great loving breast.

Sorrow and Joy clasp their hands as they wander
Down to the gateway that leads over yonder :—
Joy enters joyfully : Grief turns away—
Her home is not there where the sun shines for aye.
So these tear-troubled souls, when they come to the door,
Will be transfigured, and tears fall no more.
    Lover and Helper ! give them sweet home-rest :
    Pillow their heads on Thy great loving breast.

Spirit of Love ! heal these hearts that are breaking ;
Fill them with Heaven, whether sleeping or waking—
Joy at the noontide and Peace in the night,
Sweet Hope when the morning floods life with its light :
And when earth disappears, and the chamber grows dim,
Take them where Love fills the soul to the brim.
    Lover and Helper ! give them sweet home-rest :
    Pillow their heads on Thy great loving breast.

THE MAGI AND THE STAR

THE sky was overcast, the winds were chill ;
Strange lights chased shadows over vale and hill ;
And Melchior, lone watcher of the night,
His white beard gleaming in the fitful light,
Sat silent, prayerful, in his stone-cold tower,
When, lo, the black clouds parted at the hour
    Of midnight—and afar
      He saw the Star !

The sun went down in beauty, but the night
Grew dark with tempest : not a ray of light
Touched soothingly old Kaspar's snow-white hair
The while he knelt, and watched, and waited there
In his cold cave—with Faith and Hope his dower—
When, lo, the black clouds parted at the hour
    Of midnight—and afar
      He saw the Star !

Beyond the tumult of the upper Nile
Balthasar walked, and dreamed of God, the while
Dark storm-clouds, gathering on the mountain peaks,
Gave sudden speech, as when Jehovah speaks—

137

The great hills echoing its wondrous power—
When, lo, the black clouds parted at the hour
   Of midnight—and afar
    He saw the Star!

———

The sunset-hour was burning in the west:
Three dusty pilgrims, sadly needing rest,
Rode down the winding way to Bethlehem
To find the King—the King of kings to them:
And, lo, the Star which they had seen before
Stood flashing there above His stable door!

"Hail to the King!" the happy Wise Men cried:
"Hail to the King!" the door flew open wide,—
And there, upon a bed of fragrant hay,
The infant Jesus with sweet Mary lay,
Warm wrapped within the whitest, softest fleece—
The King, the Wonderful, the Prince of Peace.

And the angels sang,—
   "Glory to God in the highest, and on earth
   Peace, good will to men."

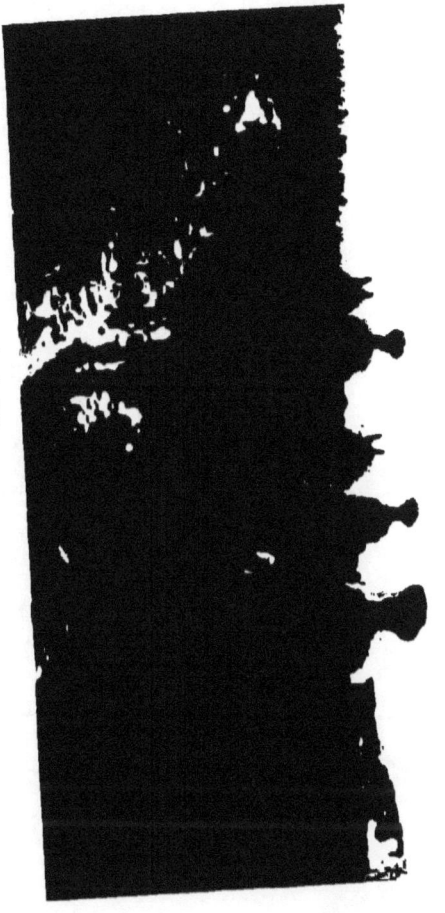

And, lo, the Star . . . .
Stood flashing 'mere above His stable door.

ADOWN THE FLASHING STREAM

A CHARADE

I GLIDE adown the flashing stream
Serenely in my First;
I trail my lines for yellow bream,
Of fish nor best nor worst :
And when I of Sahara dream,
I quench my dreamy thirst.

When every breezy summer dell
Is full of frozen dreams,
I sometimes deem it passing well
To mass the sun's warm beams,—
And in a corner of my cell
Ah! how my Second gleams!

The axis of the spinning earth
Extends from pole to pole,
And has since morning had its birth :
Withdraw it, and a hole
Of mighty length and breadth and girth
Will need my strengthening Whole.

SONG OF THE SUMMER WIND

I 'LL hie away from my native shade,
    Over the mountain and through the glade,
Rustling the leaves with my feathery tread,
And breathing perfume o'er the violets' bed,—
            Ha, ha! away, away!

I 'll ruffle the face of the crystal lake,
And laugh at the eddies my pinions make;
I 'll perch my foot on the swallow's wing,
And, sailing along, will gaily sing,—
            Ha, ha! away, away!

I 'll climb the hill on its ladder of trees,
With a tip of my cap to the lumbering bees,
While the golden grain, as I pass along,
Will bend to list to my morning song,—
            Ha, ha! away, away!

I 'll fan the cheek and the burning brow
Of one dearly loved, but dying now,
And waft her gentle spirit home
To a land of rest, no more to roam,—
            Far, far away, away!

SONG OF THE SUMMER WIND

I 'll away with the heart of the barefoot boy,
The king of the brook and the minnows coy ;
I 'll kiss the lips of the laughing girls—
Play hide-and-seek in their tumbled curls,—
Ha, ha! away, away!

And then how cheerily upward I 'll fly
To sweep the clouds from the summer sky,
And bid the moon, in the stilly night,
Bless loving hearts with her tender light,—
Ha, ha! away, away!

SONG

Dewdrop.—" I 'M a little Dewdrop,
    Round and bright and clear,
    Born among the shadows :
    Morning found me here
    Lying on a rose-leaf,
    Dreaming of the star
    That came from heaven to kiss me—
    Came, oh ! so very far !
As for life, 't will be scarcely a minute :
    The naughty sun drinks us all up !
Before we can fairly begin it,
    He gathers us into his cup !
Ah me ! all our brightness he drinks from his cup !"

Fairy.—" I 'm a little Fairy,
    Living in a dell,
    Light of foot, and airy,
    Beautiful as well ;
    But when I am sixteen
    I 'll be a fairy belle :
    Then who will want to kiss me ?
    Can anybody tell ?
But list to those sweet bells a minute (! ! !)
    The fairies in Elf-land at play !
I hear their clear songs from the spinet—
    A signal to hasten away :
Good-bye ! all we fairies must vanish away !"

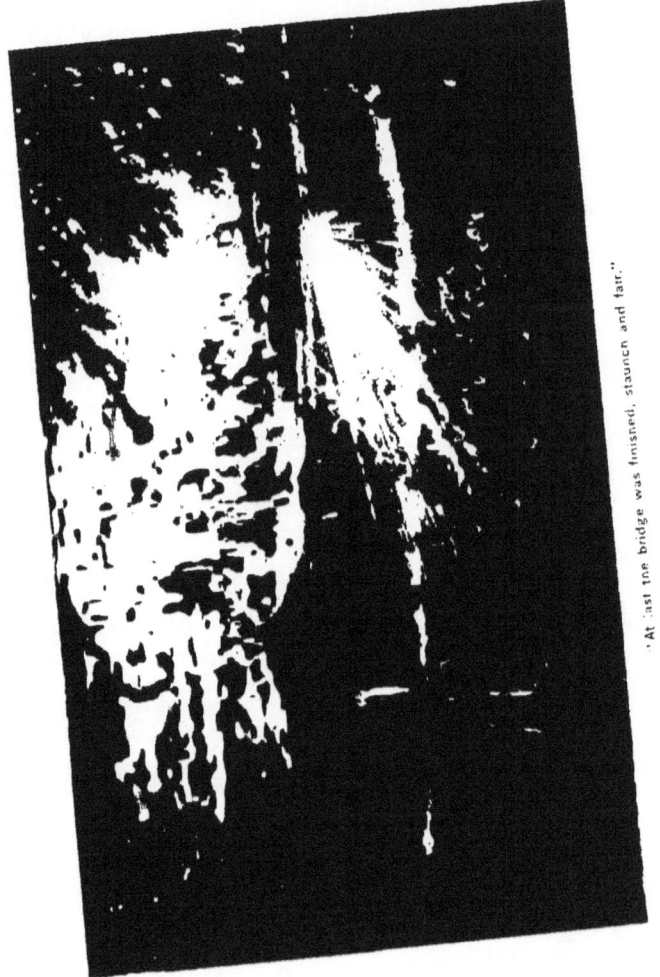

"At last the bridge was finished, staunch and fair."

THE SUNSET BRIDGE

A BREEZY upland, where the winds of all the
    sweet Septembers
  Had stayed their velvet-sandalled feet for rest,
To watch the sunset fires grow brighter from the latent
    embers
  Their wings had fanned and fashioned in the west
To molten towers and turrets;—surely every one remem-
    bers
  The sunset city that he loved the best,
  And hopes sometime to be its humble guest.

A lone old man, a sad and trembling pilgrim, bent and
    hoary,
  A worn-out relic of the vanished years,
The last of a long line of sturdy yeomen, whose quaint
    story
  Would weight the listening eyes with listening tears,
Toiled slowly up the beaten pathway, till the sunset glory
  Broke full upon his vision, and his fears
  Gave place to music strange to mortal ears.

He looked beyond the valley and the river—heard the
    singing;
  Loved voices silenced long ago were there.

He saw the silver bells of heaven swinging   heard them
    ringing ;
  Their music melted on the vibrant air.
He saw the blessed angels beck'ning to him—saw them
    bringing
  The golden wire, and weaving it with care.
  At last the bridge was finished, staunch and fair.

And while the soft, sweet winds were o'er the sleepy
    upland blowing,
  The dear Lord sent angelic hands to guide
The timid, footsore pilgrim to the home where he was
    going,
  Dry shod, across the cold, dark, silent tide.

To-day I see the ghostly waters, bridgeless, ever flowing
  Between us and the near-far other side—
  Unlike the evening when the old man died.

FOR A BIRTHDAY CALENDAR

THE way is long, O Friends!
    But it is sweet, so sweet,
To wander hand in hand
    Where overhead the swaying branches meet,
And birds sing joyous songs, by soft winds fanned,
    And velvet grasses kiss your wayworn feet;
For just beyond you, where the river bends,
You 'll find the summer-time that never ends.

149

FACES FROM WONDERLAND [1]

WHEN Rip and Schneider left the cottage door,
   The night was gruesome, and its stormy wrath
Was pitiless : the twain came back no more.
   They turned their footsteps to the mountain path
Their feet had trodden many a sunny day,
   To find it black with darkness,—every gnome
A lightning-lighted fiend, that led the way
   To dreamless slumber—ne'er to dreams of home.

So in this Wonderland : I sometimes think
   These Tritons once were driven from their homes
(By some tempestuous Gretchen) when in drink,
   And, guided hither by the wily gnomes,
Were put to sleep—a stony, dreamless sleep—
   A sleep that knows no waking : and we see
Their sightless eyeballs gazing o'er the deep—
   Unconscious watchers of the restless sea.

Take not thy way along this tragic shore
   When Night's bat wings enwrap thee, fold on fold,
For should these sleepers rouse themselves once more,
   The world would say,—This man was overbold !

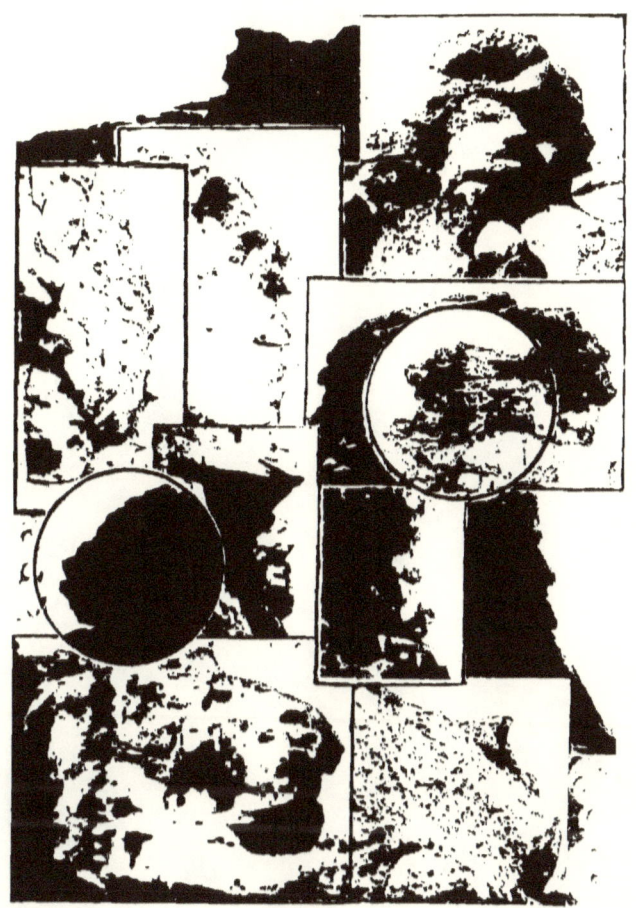

"A stony, dreamless sleep"—

O THE CHILDREN

THE children—O the children!—
    How dark the world and gloomy,
How wide and cold and roomy,
    To the mother's loving heart,
Did not the breezes waft her
The songs and merry laughter
    Of the blessed, blessed children!

The children—O the children!—
How the sun would pale his glory,
And the beautiful in story
    Die out of all the lands,
Could they not hear us calling,
When the twilight dews are falling,
    Come home, come home, O children!

The children—O the children!—
Very sweet the sacred pages,
Floating down through all the ages,
    Telling of the Christ-child born
Where the mild-eyed oxen ponder,
With a sort of wistful wonder,
    O'er the Prince of all the children!

The children—O the children!—
See them blood-red roses strowing
In the path where Christ is going
   To Jerusalem the doomed :
See them wave their cool green banners!
Hear them shout their glad hosannas
   To the Saviour of the children!

A TWISTED THING

IN a whimsical curve of the grass-grown road,
   Just over beyond the spruces,
Lies a moss-embroidered watering-trough,
   Brimful of the limpid juices
Distilled from the heart of the hill above
   By the gnomes that toil thereunder:
I can hear the rush of their elfin feet,
   And their echo-gnome-ic thunder.

This watering-trough is the quaintest thing!
   'T was carved with an axe or hatchet
In the crudest way, with the rudest blows—
   I doubt if the world can match it.
The tooth of time, or the axe, has made
   A notch in the farther corner,
Where many a barefoot girl has drank,
   And many a Jacky Horner.

The dear old log is a twisted thing—
   But it holds the sweetest water
That ever was drank by beast or bird,
   Or quaffed by son or daughter:
And yesterday, after forty years,
   I searched until I found it—

A doubtful chance, for the grasses' arms
  Were lovingly clasped around it.

A face looked up from the mimic sea—
  Alas! 't was not the old one!
But the yellow frog at the farther end
  Was the very same old bold one,—
A pop-eyed fiend, who never winked
  When I bent to quaff the nectar;—
If it was n't that same old "crazy quilt,"
  It must have been his spectre.

And Nell, O Nell, do you mind the day
  You knelt down close beside me—
I never shall forget it, sweet,
  Whatever may betide me—
And we bent above this tell-tale cup,
  Reflecting untold blisses,
And saw two faces looking up,
  And kisses chasing kisses?

A brown-faced, blue-eyed, barefoot girl—
  The angels—how they love her!
A barefoot boy with bleeding feet,
  Her constant, gray-haired lover—
Will search the paths of heaven some day
  For such a nook as this is,
And find, perchance, this very pool,
  With all its wealth of kisses.

BLUE EYES

BLUE eyes, laughing merrily!
 Why so sparkling? Verily,
Two quivers full of bristling arrows art thou,
 Waiting for thy bow;—
For thy bow hath many strings,
And the arrows that it flings
At random, lay some palpitating heart, now,
 Bleeding, thou must know,
 Laughing blue eyes!
 Chaffing blue eyes!
 At thy shoe-tips low.

Blue eyes! tender, dutiful,
Full of love-light, beautiful,
Why dost thou ever wave thy long brown lashes—
 Wave them in my face?
For they reach me in my dreams,
Interlaced with sunny gleams
From the queenly soul that seems
Forever weaving round me love's light meshes—
 Captive to thy grace,
 Truest blue eyes!
 Bluest blue eyes!
 Fairest of thy race!

157

BLUE EYES

Blue eyes! once so cheerfully,
　Now, alas! so tearfully
Beyond thy narrow prison barriers peering,
　　Longing for one word,—
　Come I whence the cannons' boom
　Told of many a hero's tomb
By Chicamauga's crimson tide appearing :
　　　Deeply thou wert stirred,
　　　　Tearful blue eyes!
　　　　Fearful blue eyes!
　　　Trembling like a bird!

Blue eyes! greet me cheerily,
　Coming back so wearily,
Thy love-light ever on my proud heart beaming
　　As stars beam on the sea :
　Nestle closely to my breast,
　While I gaze, supremely blest,
　Down thy crystal depths in quest
Of love's young dream—for surely thou art dreaming!
　　　Dreaming, too, of me—
　　　　Mistful blue eyes!
　　　　Wistful blue eyes!
　　　Sweet as sweet can be!

158

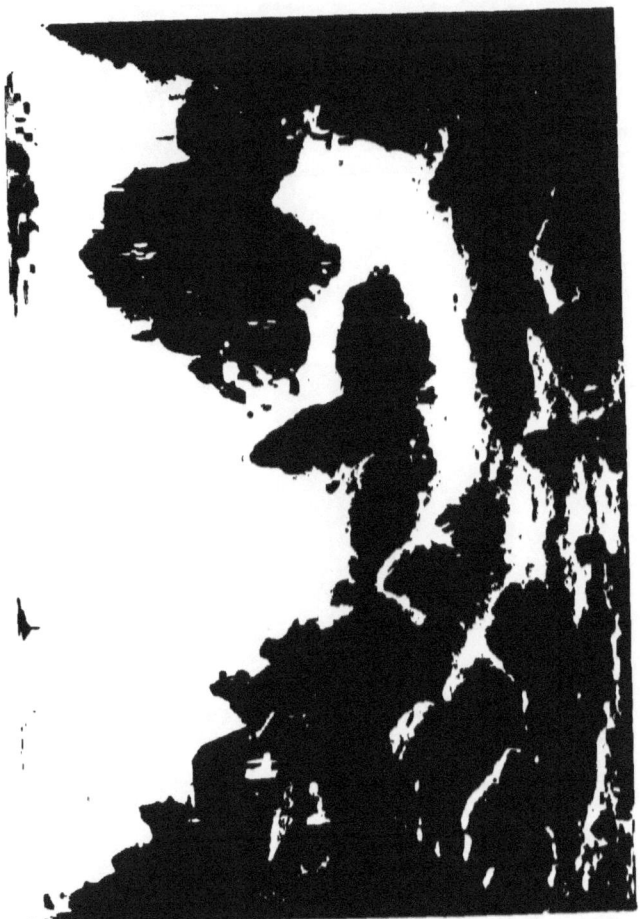

BRIGHT PASSACONAWAY

LIKE some fair castle on the Rhine,
    Or Lurlei of the rock,
That overlooks the fields of wine,
    The shepherd's homely flock,
You stand, bright Passaconaway !
    Upon the cliffs of York.

We hear the wind about your eaves
    Blow inward from the sea ;
Sometimes a sea-sad tale it weaves,
    A song without a key,—
But still, bright Passaconaway !
    It wrings no tears from thee.

When past the Nubble's jagged nose
    Sweeps Equinoctial thunder,
And some great vessel, plunging, goes
    The seething waters under,
You gaze, calm Passaconaway !
    With eyes brimful of wonder.

You stand serene upon the heights
    Where night's soft winds are blowing :

Your flashing eyes, your hundred lights,
  A burning beacon glowing,
Invite us, Passaconaway !
  To where good cheer is flowing.

HÉLÈNE

UNDER that snow-white sheet she lies—
   Hélène my beautiful! Hélène my true!
Softly the morning breaks over the skies,
  Softly regretful stars kiss her Adieu;—
     Lies she there seeming
     So blissfully dreaming,—
  Fragrant her ripe lips as breath of the morn,—
     No one shall lisp her
     Name even in whisper:
She's roaming where fairy-land fancies are born!

Clustering clouds of dark, passionate hair
  Frown back the curious beams of the sun:
Hidden but meagrely, shapely and rare,
  Round, white, soft mysteries wait to be won;—
     Seemingly bolder,
     One Parian shoulder,
  Purity's self, dims the pillow below—
     While, thrown above her
     Head (who could but love her!)
A round arm lies white as the shimmering snow!

Parting as clouds part when summer winds blow,
  Heavenly wonders unveiling above,—

HÉLÈNE

So part the gauze-clouds, revealing below
  Opaline mountains in gardens of love :—
    Soft undulations,
    Like music's vibrations
Coursing light-footed the silvery strings,
    Seem like the ocean
    In jubilant motion,
Rocking its burden of beautiful things !

Waking as wake the young birds in their nests,
  Baby Nell opens her wondering eyes—
Climbs where the lush mountains bear on their crests
  Strawberries ripe as the ruddiest skies :—
    There, among treasures
    In bountiful measures,
Roguish-eyed, cherry-lipped, pink-footed Nell
    Drinks from a chalice
    The king in his palace
Might barter his crown for, and barter it well !

THE REAPER

IT was so warm that summer day!
Yet the hill winds would play with the bearded
    grasses,
And with miserly glee toss the gleaming masses
Of billowy grain, in the sun's broad splendor,
Or touch them with kisses soft and tender,—
    While over the drowsy lea
  Came the Reaper's song, like a dirge of doom,
  Mantling the bended heads with gloom
    As it swept o'er the rippling sea ;—
    And the Reaper's eyes were dim,
For at every swing of his circling blade,
The pitying air bore off to the glade
    A bar of his cradle hymn :
    " In spring we sow—in autumn reap—
    'T is time for song—no time to weep—
    Sleep, my beloved !—sleep—sleep—sleep !"
    And the watchful grasses whispered, " Sleep !"

So when on fields of strife pursuing Night
Hurls down the west the blood-red orb of light,
A thousand forms, late sweeping o'er the plain
Where gleaming sickles shook the crimson rain,

165

Lie scattered, like the tempest-riven leaves—
Columbia's martyrs, Liberty's dear sheaves:
And while in silent chambers calm they rest,
A grateful country folds them to her breast.

   From yonder hillside, where the trees
   Keep watch above the voiceless village,
     And chant their morning melodies
   O'er homes no vandal hand may pillage,
A hundred sheaves will spring to heaven's wide dome
When the Great Reaper shouts his Harvest Home!

"A boy who gives no quarter (but takes one when he can')"

THE VERY BIGGEST BOY

"DO you want to see the biggest, yes, the very big-
    gest boy—
A boy that Big 's no name for, his mother's wildest joy?
A boy that 's tall 's a flagstaff, as deep as any well,
As wide as any church door, and merry as a bell?
                    Here 's your Man!

" Do you want to see the brightest, cutest little (no, *big !*)
    boy—
A boy that 's up to snuff, you bet (but not to maccoboy)?
A boy that is so very old, and knows so very much,
He can tell you how old Holland was taken by the Dutch?
                    Here 's your Man!

" Do you want to see the strongest boy—a chap to do
    and dare—
A boy that tracks the rabbits and the foxes to their lair?
A boy that whistles, whittles, and swaps jack-knives every
    day—
Who 's as sweet as any daisy, or as pinks in a bouquet?
                    Here 's your Man!

" Do you want to see the bravest boy, who 's always in
    the van—
A boy who gives no quarter (but takes one when he can !)?

Who swims the rivers, hunts the bees, and never tires
   of play—
Who never growls, or sheds a tear, no matter what you say?
                 Here's your Man!

"Do you want to see a boy with a head that's full of
   brains?
(Just look this way a minute—charge you nothing for
   your pains!)
A boy that surely knows what's what from morning
   until night,
And never fights a battle but he battles for the right?
                 Here's your Man!

"If you wish to see the biggest boy, the brightest, and
   the best;
The boy that says his prayers (or ought to!) when he
   goes to rest;
The boy that means, when President ('t will not be very
   long!)
To hustle in 'The good time coming,' righting all the
   wrong—
                Here's your Man!"

IS IT NOT STRANGE

IS it not strange how stealthily To-day
   Slips into Yesterday and glides away?—
I'en while you sleep he steals adown the stair,
Unbolts the ponderous door, and goes—you know not
      where.

No rumbling of great iron wheels is heard—
   The pulses of the dreamer are not stirred—
When the long train of flying Yesterdays
Halts at your midnight door—then speeds its wonted
      ways.

It leaves a youthful traveller at your gate
   To take the place of him who could not wait ;—
The young To-day walks in and climbs the tower,
While yet the brazen hammers forge the spectral hour.

Morn after morn, with hand close clasped in hand,
   To-day and I stroll through the dewy land,
And climb the breezy hills, through shaded ways,
To list the echoes of the train of Yesterdays.

But, ah ! how much of hope, and love, and light
Goes with the chain that coils into the night !

IS IT NOT STRANGE

I plead for passage, but I plead in vain—
I part with each To-day at threshold of the train.

I 'm stranded on the hills;—but some fair morn
The bobolinks will sing among the corn,—
And happy children in their happy play
Will say in loving tones,—*He left us yesterday.*

THE RIVER BEAUTIFUL.[12]

SILENCE sleeps in thy valley,
  O beautiful stream!
O wayward and mystical river!
  Dreaming a pleasant dream
As the sunbeams on thy murmuring ripples quiver,
    And talking in his sleep—
    His sleep so sound and deep!

Dreaming of maidens roaming
  Thy banks along,
And of jets of sparkling laughter
  Bursting from waves of song
That must die away on the shores of the dim Hereafter—
    That peaceful, voiceless sea,
    Kin to eternity!

Silence hath myriad voices,
  O gleaming tide!
And from thine enchanting valley,
  Radiant in its pride,
They come to the cliff where the poet stands, and shall he
    Interpret them to thee,
    Under this old pine tree?

" Beautiful, beautiful river!"
   The old pine sighs :
And the wrinkled, gray old ledges,
   Tears in their mossy eyes,
Toss back an echo from their jagged edges
     To that lone sentinel
     Guarding the valley well.

Fondly the tall pine watches
   Thy narrow bed,
Fearing some morn to miss thee,
   Beautiful silver thread !
And ere the glooming he sends his shadow to kiss thee
     A soft and sweet Good-night
     Till morning's rosy light.

Maples with crimson blushing
   Far down below,
And distant hillsides climbing,
   Changed to a golden glow,—
All lend a tongue to that mysterious chiming,
     Deep as the sounding sea,
     Deep as their love for thee !

Blending in sweetest music,
   The tinkling feet
Of rivulets down-rushing
   Dance to thy silver sheet,
While the rapt sun through golden rifts is flushing

Thy face with heaven's own light :
O dream too brief, too bright !

" Beautiful, beautiful river !"
  The old pine sighs :
In the silence my heart replieth, —
  " Daughter of earth and skies,
Farewell ! but at last, when my weary spirit flieth
    Beyond the chiming stars,
    May my eyes unclasp their bars
To see thy placid waters calmly flowing
Out from the Burning Throne, and down the valley
    glowing !"

Y^E OLD STONE WALL,

"OCTO^{BRE} 14th 1796—
Begun ye Stone Wall round ye Garden Plotte
Below ye Barn—2 Akers thereabouts"—
    'T is fairly legible, with here a blot,
And there a hasty scratch where "plotte" had been
    misspelled,—
And then—a hundred years the yellow "record" held:

    Thanks to the dry old garret, where the rain
        Could find no loophole; to the old hair trunk,
    Its brass nails hid beneath the trash of years,
        And dust, and spiders' broidery—a bunk,
Secure and silent as King Shufu's mighty tomb,
Wherein the "record" slept amid the unvexed gloom.

        (At the breakfast-table)

    "The very durablest fence in all the world,"
        Said Uncle Jerry, "is a *good* stone wall:
    If built as 't should be, 't lasts f'rever,—
        'N' I do' know any better time 'an the fall
To start it 'long. These frosty nights make workin'
    days,
'N' when you put a big stone in its place, it stays."

178

" 'T will look so nice and strong," said Grandma
   Brawn :
   " I like to see the broad-backed, heavy stones,
I' the bottom layer, bearing the lesser ones
   So sturdily, with neither frowns nor groans :
They mind me of the burdens we should gladly bear
For those we love—and others—here and everywhere."

   " And if the wall is built of great big stones,"
      Said black-eyed Nell, " 't will be so nice to climb!
And when the garden 's full of sweet green corn,
      And flowers, and fruit, in the bright summer-time,
And vines are running over all the garden wall,
We 'll play it 's Eden—I 'll be Eve before the fall !"

   " Won't it be jolly fun," said little Ben,
      " When all the cows come swinging home at night,
To see their noses there above the wall,
      Their soft mouths watering for a juicy bite
Of all that corn and beans?—*I* would n't be a cow
For anything !——*No, sir!*—at least, I would n't now !"

   " There is no doubt of it," said Gran'ther Brawn,—
      " The best of fences *is* a *good* stone wall ;
And there is not a farm in all the town
      With rocks more plenty within easy call :
Let us be duly thankful !——Now to the field we go—
A month's hard work before us, e'en till the driving
      snow."

And so the old stone wall was built around
   " Y" Garden Plotte :" its massive stones to-day
Are proudly standing there, erect and firm —
   Some lichens mingled with their iron gray—
While all the blithesome, strong, and willing hearts and
      hands
That built this deathless wall now dwell in other lands.

" A beautiful Nowoman's hand
Driving seventeen dripping sea-horses "—

NOMAN'S LAND

*S*OMEWHERE there's a wonderful country :
  Do you think it lies over the deep?
It may be far off in the mountains ;
  An island, perhaps, fast asleep ;—
Just fancy !—perhaps up above us,
  Beyond the bright stars and the blue,
Great rivers and lakes and green valleys
  Are waiting for me and for you.

But how can we get there, I wonder !
  No boatman will take us to-day ;
No tally-ho leaves for the mountains ;
  Some siren would lead us astray
If we were to start off together—
  No compass or chart to our hand—
In the darkest or sunniest weather,
  To find that invisible land.

The road to that strangest of countries—
  Do you know that I saw it last night?
It may only be travelled when shadows
  Can dance hand in hand with the light.
I lay on the rocks by the ocean
  And looked out far over the sea,

When the great Harvest Moon took a notion
  To come up and hob-nob with me.

In an instant a flashing of silver—
  A few low commands from the Queen
A crowd of the nimblest of workmen—
  Wide layers of mystical sheen—
Great rollers in rapid succession
  Drawn steadily in from the sea
By the steadiest teams of sea-horses——
  And the road was all ready for me.

Was there ever a vision so splendid ?—
  A beautiful Nowoman's hand
Driving seventeen dripping sea horses
  Post haste from the far Noman's Land !
She drove to the rocks like a whirlwind—
  She whistled and beckoned to me :
Oh ! who could withstand a Nowoman !
  She drove like a flash to the sea.

What I saw on that nocturnal journey—
  What I heard when we reached Noman's Land—
The Nochildren's silvery laughter
  While sifting the silvery sand ;
The bonniest Nomaidens romping
  With clouds of the airiest elves,—
I must never reveal—it 's a secret !—
  You must go there and see for yourselves !

THE JOY-BELLS RING [13]

THE sunlight seems less bright and clear,
   The dreary winter winds more drear,
More frequent now the blinding tear,
     Since they are gone.

The voices of the birds are hushed :
The woods, erstwhile with beauty flushed,
Stand all unrobed—their spirits crushed—
     Since they are gone.

The music that illumed the air,
And made the world so blithe and fair,
Is voiceless now : its home is where
     The loved are gone.

Two nobler souls ne'er crossed the stream :
I saw the boatman, in my dream,
Row gently, as the sunset-gleam
     Bathed them in gold.

Bright forms intangible were there
To help them up the landing stair,
While unseen music filled the air—
     Their welcome home.

And now they hear the joy-bells ring,
They hear the " Well done " of the King,
And haste with flying feet to bring
    Their earth-born gifts.

Here loving hearts and weary feet
Walk slowly, sadly down the street
That leads to where the two worlds meet—
    The river's brim.

Adown the vista of the years
I see that pathway paved with tears,
But know its footsore pilgrims' fears
    Will end in home.

"Dear tired Mother Earth has gone to sleep."

ASLEEP

DEAR tired Mother Earth has gone to sleep:
   Walk tiptoe through her chamber lest she waken!
Her children faithful watch above her keep,
   While she with slumber sweet is overtaken.

Not long ago a thousand tender ferns
   Spread over her their wealth of dew-spun laces,
And nestled close to her warm heart, where burns
   The fire that kindles Spring-time's sylvan graces.

And when the blessed Mother longed for rest,
   How soothingly the little slender grasses
Threw all their soft green arms across her breast:
   No wintry blast shall touch her as it passes!

ASLEEP

The maples watched her with a beaming smile
   When proud October covered them with glory,
And gladly doffed their royal robes, the while
   With them they made her bed—the old sweet story!

And yesterday all day the longing sky
   Bent lovingly and wistfully above her,
While soft white kisses—oh, so tenderly!
   With sweet insistance placed her under cover.

UNDER THE OLD ELM

AND this is June :—these overhanging boughs
    Invite us—nay, entice us—to a rest
Upon this soft, green, fragrant mother-breast,
Where we may watch the sweet home-coming cows
Wind down the hill, and listen to the vows
    We have no right to hear from that small nest
    That swings above us, while the waning west
Breathes benedictions on our throbbing brows.
        Here we will dream the twilight hours away
        Beneath this ample firmament of leaves,
        And listen to the whirr of unseen wings
        Within the shadows, while the soft airs play
        The songs our mother sung, that time nor thieves
        Can filch from mem'ry's storehouse—Hark ! she
            sings !

SPRING IS COMING

SNOW in the meadow and snow on the hill ;
  Snow in the woodlands, deep, breathless, and still ;
Snow on the pond and the ice-covered brook,
And all the world over, wherever we look ; –
But voices are calling from over the ridge—
Let us hasten away across valley and bridge,
  And find what 's in store for our ears and our eyes,
  On the hills, in the woods, ere the glory-light dies.

Were ever the steps of the west winds so fleet ?
Were ever soft winds from the far-lands so sweet ?
  Just list to the stories they bring from Lahore,
  Japan, and the islands they 'll visit no more—
No more till they circle the earth on the wing,
And come again, o'er the same path, with the Spring :
  Soft measures they sing, and the whispering pines
  Repeat to our ears their melodious lines.

But, hark ! on the hill over there in the west
I hear the hoarse caw of the crows : 't is the best
  The black fellows can do to express their delight,
  For they never could sing much : black cannot be
    white !

And just now, in that old hollow tree on ahead,
A drowsy red squirrel turned over in bed,
  And, yawning, said, " Mother, wake up in a wink !
  For the beautiful Spring-time is coming, I think."

And if we stand still where the snow is not deep,
We shall feel the warm ground where the daffodils sleep
  Just trembling and aching to open the door
  And let the imprisoned ones leap to the fore :
And all the small people that live in the ground
Have slept their bright eyes out, and long for the sound
  Of the feet of the Spring, as she comes o'er the hills
  To touch the spring-locks and unfetter the rills.

Did you see me just now put my ear to the bark
Of that great maple tree ?—Well, inside, in the dark,
  You can hear, step by step, up the ladder, the floods
  Of sweet juices climb sturdily up to the buds :
And—oh, marvel of Spring-time ! oh, marvel of birth !—
Every wonderful germ in the womb of the earth
  Springs to light, clothed in beauty and gladness, to
    sing
  With ineffable joy the swift coming of Spring.

THE SPINNING-WHEEL AT REST

THE DAY'S WORK DONE

ALL day we heard it humming
  Like softly falling snow,
And busy feet were coming,
  Going, to and fro,
One hand upon the whirling wheel,
One playing with the whirring steel.

All day we heard it spinning :
  Its song of love and cheer
Was sweet from the beginning :
  But listen ! you shall hear
Another voice, as clear and low
As songs from roses when they blow.

All day the sweet-voiced spinner
  And her wheel sing soft and low :
Warm love-light burns within her—
  Her cheeks like roses glow :
The tea-kettle takes up the song,
And shakes his cap with laughter long.

194

NOTES

[1] *The Old Stone Bridge*—Page 23—A bridge over the picturesque Ashuelot River, in the town of Gilsum, N. H.

[2] *The Return*—Page 41—In the early years of the Rebellion, enlistments for the Union army were usually made for "three years."

[3] *Speed the Going—Welcome the Coming*—Page 51—During the years immediately succeeding the Rebellion—"the reconstruction period"—the newspapers of the South were full of (perhaps pardonable) bitterness; and the "broken words" of the dying year were but echoes from their editorial and news columns.

[4] *A Portrait from the Sea*—Page 76—An exact reproduction of a pebble found by the author among hundreds of tons of variegated stones on Pebbly Beach, York, Me.

[5] *Anniversary Poem*—Page 101—Read at the celebration of the seventy-fifth anniversary of Thetford (Vt.) Academy, June 28, 1894.

[6] Page 106—Hiram Orcutt, LL. D., principal of the academy from 1843 to 1856. He was present on this occasion, at the age of eighty, in good health, and made an entertaining after-dinner speech at the banquet.

[7] *Two Apples*—Page 111—The illustrations of this poem are used by the kind permission—"Eve," of the Berlin Photographic Co., of New York, and "Tell," of E. C. Allen & Co., of Augusta, Me.

[8] *A Hundred Years Ago*—Page 119—Written for the Centennial Anniversary of the Congregational Church, in Newport, N. H., Oct. 28, 1879.

[9] Page 119—In June, 1766, eight young men, five having families, arrived in Newport for permanent settlement. The next morning (Sunday) they met under a pine tree for worship. Since that day the Congregationalists have never permitted a Sunday to pass without public religious services.

[10] *Spirit of Love*—Page 136—This hymn is adapted to the tune "Fading, still fading"—which will explain certain peculiarities of metrical construction.

[11] *Faces from Wonderland*—Page 150—All these faces are exact photographic reproductions of actual rocks on the magnificent coast of York Beach, Me., and all within a few minutes' walk of each other. And there are others. It is indeed a Wonderland for those who have "eyes to see."

[12] *The River Beautiful*—Page 175—"Sugar River," at Newport, N. H., the exquisite stream that leads the waters of Sunapee Lake to the Connecticut, a distance of twenty miles;—so called by the early settlers because of the great maple forests on its tributary hills.

[13] *The Joy-Bells Ring*—Page 185—Mr. and Mrs. William E. Stevens, of Portland, Me.—long residents of Concord, N. H.

DATE DUE

GAYLORD			PRINTED IN U S A

www.ingramcontent.com/pod-product-compliance
Lightning Source LLC
Chambersburg PA
CBHW030539040726
47497CB00008B/2514